Historical Duos

Extraordinary Partnerships That Shaped
History

PL Thomas

Table of Contents

Introduction

The pages of history have been written by remarkable people who have stood the test of time. We all remember names like Albert Einstein, the physicist, and the tragic story of Anne Frank that has moved everybody's hearts. How many relevant names could we add to that list? They were all extraordinary people indeed, but did you know that many of them weren't alone when they achieved greatness? Many famous people had a partner who was key to fulfilling their goals or fighting the challenges with them.

Many renowned names are usually credited for accomplishing spectacular tasks, but the truth is they had backup. Very few can say they became successful on their own. There was another name that remained in the shadows. We won't discuss why only one of them became popular and got the laurels of glory. We just aim to take a look around some of the greatest figures of all time and see who stood beside them or behind and was later forgotten. We want to know who they joined forces with to leave their indelible mark in history, although we only see one pair of footprints.

If we think of an adventure mate or a team worker, we prefer someone we have a lot in common with, someone we like. It doesn't always work like that, though. It is surprising to find out that many of the people we are going to learn about had to work with people they didn't actually like. Sometimes, the perfect match isn't your soulmate but your nemesis. Duos aren't strictly an equivalent of a couple.

It is interesting to pay closer attention to the original meaning of the word duo. It isn't just any pair of two things. The word is taken from the Latin term "duo," which refers to a unique set of two components. Its existence isn't just a sum of those two elements. Instead, they get together to create a new, different entity. This means that no matter how much each member of the duo tried, neither of them would have been able to do the same thing alone as they could accomplish together. Together as a duo, they are moved by a sui generis synergy.

We have learned about famous duos in different historical periods and realms. We have heard of Romeo and Juliet, Bonnie and Clyde, or Queen Elizabeth and King Ferdinand, but how many know that Nehru and Gandhi worked together for the independence of India? Would it be possible to talk about Frida Kahlo without thinking of Diego Rivera?

This book presents the stories of duos that made invaluable contributions to change the world and have left enduring legacies that persist in the present.

Chapter 1:

Academic Duos

Voltaire and Émilie du Châtelet (1700s)

The 18th century wasn't a friendly time for women in science. Not many of them had access to education, particularly higher education. A genius of philosophy and a maid of Louis XIV's court seems an impossible match, and yet, Western scientific tradition is based on many accomplishments of this couple.

The name François-Marie Arouet doesn't sound very familiar because history has remembered him by his pseudonym: Voltaire. He was one of the most prolific, prominent, and subversive philosophers and writers of the 18th century. His work, among other philosophers and scientists, set the basis for the greatest change in humankind's way of seeing the world and inaugurated the thinking movement known as the Enlightenment. He was one of the minds that brought light to Europe and all the Western world.

Voltaire was born on November 21, 1694, in Paris. He belonged to a typical middle-class family during the rise of the French bourgeoisie. By then, people of his class struggled with the lack of civil and political rights.

He had a thorough education but was mainly embedded with religious beliefs, though it only served to increase his skepticism. He was deeply impressed by the turbulent environment of the last years of Louis XIV's rule, the atrocities of war, and the religious persecutions of the Huguenots. That must have influenced his ideas against absolutism and religious intolerance, which was later reflected in his work.

Even though he studied law and had a job as a secretary in the public office, he wanted to be a writer. He became a popular poet and playwright. However, his witty pen led him into trouble when he mocked the Duc d'Orléans, the Regent of France. Voltaire was imprisoned in the Bastille, a place for political prisoners. He had some personal reasons to claim liberty of freedom and speech.

That wasn't the first time he was punished for expressing rebellious ideas. He was famous in the French courts for professing deism, which was severely censored by the predominant Catholics. He was eventually banished from his country and exiled to England, a country Voltaire personally admired for being the land of flourishing commerce and progress, freedom, and liberalism.

Some years later, he came back to France as an established author and published *Lettres Philosophiques*, a landmark in the history of Western thinking. It is a collection of fictional letters that serve to expose his ideas about the real purpose of life: It isn't the pursuit of eternal life after death through penitence but to achieve happiness through progress, guided by reason.

Voltaire was a brilliant mind who didn't shine alone. He was lit up by an extraordinary partner. She wasn't only brilliant but also courageous and eager to change the society of her time. Her name was Émilie.

Her full name was Gabrielle-Émilie Le Tonnelier de Breteuil, Marquise du Châtelet, and she was born in 1706 in Paris. She was a member of the nobility, and being still very young, her father arranged her marriage to Marquis Florent du Châtelet, governor of Semur-en-Auxois. With this man, whom she didn't love and was almost never at home with, she had three children.

Nonetheless, she had many other businesses to attend, even though business was considered rather unfeminine at the time. She was a dedicated mathematician and physicist. This was very unusual in times when women's role in society was limited to the private sphere and the frivolous entertainments of court life.

Even though she enjoyed the banquettes and balls, she was very interested in science, particularly in the contributions of Isaac Newton to physics and math. She spent many years of her life working on the translation of his main work, *Principia Mathematica*, into French.

Unlike Voltaire, her education was achieved at home. Her father was a man of science, and he fostered his daughter's curiosity, leading her to achieve a scope most women of her time didn't. She was so keen on science that she would use her talents for math to succeed at gambling. She used the money she earned to buy more books (Lucas, 2019).

After getting married, she moved out of Paris to live with her husband and children. However, Émilie was determined to follow her many other interests and decided to go back to Paris. She was ready to break all the social—and moral—restrictive rules of the French aristocracy.

Back in Paris, she became the pupil of important mathematicians, first Pierre Louis Maupertuis and then Alexis-Claude Clairaut. She not only dedicated herself to studying and writing but also to promoting science and participation among women. She opened a research center in Cirey, and in her intellectual salons, women were invited to learn and discuss about more than dresses and jewelry.

Living in Paris, Émilie was an active participant in social gatherings at the Court and intellectual gatherings. In one of those gatherings, she met Voltaire, who was, by then, a renowned and controversial writer. They felt mutually attracted to each other immediately. Soon, they started a romantic relationship that wasn't only fueled by love or passion but by the common intellectual interests they shared.

Due to his irreverent works, Voltaire was again forced to flee Paris, but this time, he wasn't welcome in England. So, he sought shelter at the du Châtelet's chateau in Cirey-sur-Blaise, property of Émilie. The place was practically in ruins, and it had many debts, but it was a safe place to hide to avoid spending a new season at the Bastille. Voltaire used his money to restore it. The couple established themselves at the chateau in 1737 and started a life and a scientific career together that lasted 15 years.

Émilie and Voltaire felt the same passion for science and worked together on many projects. Sometimes, they engaged together in scientific contests, and other times, they competed against each other.

In 1738, the Paris Academy presented a contest that consisted of writing an essay under the title "The Propagation of Fire." On that occasion, Voltaire and Émilie took part in the competition with separate works, although both of them refuted the theory of fire being a material substance. Even though the contest was won by Leonhard Euler, Émilie and Voltaire received an honorable mention for the quality of their essays, which were published along with the other winners (Walton, 2018).

The professional relationship between Émilie and Voltaire lasted longer than their romantic affair. It was turbulent from the beginning, and both found new partners. However, the mutual respect and admiration continued, and therefore, they continued to collaborate in scientific experiments and writings.

Both scientists had a prolific life, although Émilie's works are usually less recognized. Madame du Châtelet wrote the *Institutions de Physique*, where she explained the current ideas in the field at her time with her own propositions. The book revealed the influence of Descartes and Leibniz and their contributions to correct Newton's mechanics.

Émilie also wrote important works as a translator and used some of the books to introduce her opinions about the role of women in French society. One of the books she translated was *The Fable of the Bees* by Bernard Mandeville. The story is a fable about social status differences, and Émilie used the preface to highlight the obstacles for women to achieve education and access to intellectual and public life.

Some years after Voltaire and Émilie were separated, she was working on her greatest translation work: Newton's *Principia Mathematica*. She wasn't only translating from English to French but also adding her own notes to explain or present different ideas. She was pregnant when the manuscript was ready to be sent to her teacher for revision. Emilie was 42 years old by then, a highly risky age to be pregnant in the 18th century. In 1749, while her manuscript was under review, Emilie gave birth to her daughter and died a few days later due to complications (Eschner, 2021).

Voltaire himself was in charge of having Émilie's book published in 1756. Voltaire also wrote the preface of one of the most important books of the time. It was the only translation of the *Principia Mathematica* into French for a long time.

Voltaire is recognized as one of the mentors of the Enlightenment, and his works *Dictionnaire Philosophique Portatif* (1764) and the *Questions sur l'Encyclopédie* (1770–1772) are considered part of the basis of rationalism and contemporary philosophy. His ideas against tolerance and abuse of power and his advocacy for freedom of religion and speech were inspirations for the French Revolution.

Émilie du Châtelet is less credited for her own efforts and contributions to science and her fight for a place for women in science and public life. For many, she is still one of Voltaire's lovers who helped him when he was a political fugitive. Nonetheless, Émilie was a woman who confronted every social prejudice. She not only contributed to spreading Newton's ideas in physics and Descartes and Leibniz's rationalism in Europe but also contributed to the development of science by adding her original theories and discoveries and her revolutionary ideas about society.

Marie and Pierre Curie (1800s)

During the second half of the 19th century, Europe grappled between the frenetic scientific evolution fueled by the Second Industrial Revolution and the social unrest triggered by the inequalities of capitalist society. In this world, a Polish girl who dreamed of being a scientist and a middle-class boy from Paris joined to make together some of the most important discoveries of the century and of all time, with a broad impact on all fields that endures until the present. They would give their entire life to science for the good of humankind.

Pierre Curie was born on May 15, 1859, in Paris. He was the son of a doctor who dedicated himself to educating young Pierre. He was only 18 when he was admitted as a laboratory assistant at Sorbonne, the most prestigious university in the country. By then, he had proved to be skilled in spatial geometry and obtained his *licence ès sciences* and gained his licentiateship in physics. Despite his many merits, it wasn't easy for Pierre to obtain a solid position within the university. It took him over 20 years to be assigned as a titular professor.

Among his most relevant works in the early years of his career, it is worth naming his studies on crystallography in cooperation with his brother, Jacques. Pierre applied a method to calculate the length of heat waves and developed a contribution to the study of crystals by using the laws of symmetry. That eventually led the Curie brothers to discover piezoelectricity. Later, his interests shifted to magnetism. With the invention of several instruments such as electrometers, balances, and piezoelectric crystals, among others, he discovered that substances' magnetic properties changed at a certain temperature, but he would have to work hard to demonstrate it.

During the spring of 1894, Pierre was working on his doctoral thesis. He wanted to demonstrate what was then called the Curies' law, which states—in simple words—that the magnetic attraction between bodies varies due to temperature. Pierre couldn't imagine that the beautiful Polish girl he met at the university would be his greatest support to revolutionize physics.

Her name was Maria Skłodowska, and she was born on November 7, 1867, in Warsaw, Poland. She had shown remarkable intellectual skills since she was a young girl. When she was 16, she won an important competition in Russian lycée. She dreamed of becoming a scientist, but she would have to fight against many challenges to achieve it. Maria was the fifth daughter of a poor family. Her mother died when she was still very young, and her father did what he could to hold the family together.

As a teenager, Maria had to take a job to sustain herself. She became a governess but continued to study on her own in her little free time. She wanted to be a teacher, but the economic odds prevented her from achieving higher education. One day, she finally had her chance when her sister asked Maria to join her in Paris. Maria didn't hesitate and moved to the French capital in 1891. There, she immediately entered Sorbonne.

After some time in Paris, Maria adopted French nationality and became Marie. As a student, Marie met Pierre. After a brief romance, they got married in 1895, the same year when Pierre defended his thesis to obtain a Doctor of Science degree. From then on, he continued his experiments on magnetism with his wife. The beginning of their relationship was hard since they had few resources. Their incomes barely covered their minimal expenses to live, and they didn't have enough support from the university for their research. The couple worked as researchers at the School of Chemistry and Physics in Paris and continued their studies on a recent phenomenon discovered by Henri Becquerel. Marie called it "radioactivity."

Marie noticed that a mineral called pitchblende, which contained uranium, had more radioactivity than pure uranium. It could only mean one thing: It must be a different element. It was polonium, named so on behalf of Marie's birth country. A few months later, further research proved there was one more element: radium.

Pierre dedicated himself to studying the new radiation while Marie spent most of the time trying to obtain pure radium. She had to obtain tons of pitchblende from Austria. The couple spent a lot of time carrying out experiments and observing, working with all this radioactive material, ignorant by then of the terrible damage to their health. In 1903, after many attempts and arduous work, Marie was able to isolate radium and determine its atomic place at its atomic weight of 225.93, giving it a place in the periodic table (Marie Curie, n.d.).

The couple's innovative findings earned them several prizes in 1903, including the Nobel Prize for Physics from the Royal Swedish Academy of Sciences. Pierre and Marie shared this prize for the discovery of radioactivity with Becquerel. In the speech upon receiving the prize, Pierre was careful to point out the discoveries the couple had made together and those achieved by his wife alone. He also warned about the harmful potential of scientific discoveries. Then, he said (Curie, 1905)

> It can even be thought that radium could become very dangerous in criminal hands, and here the question can be raised whether mankind benefits from knowing the secrets of Nature, whether it is ready to profit from it, or whether this knowledge will not be harmful for it. (p.76)

In 1904, Pierre was finally assigned as a titular professor in the Faculty of Sciences, and the monetary prize helped the couple overcome the economic shortages they had been struggling through for all those years. The couple had two daughters, Irène and Ève, and with a stable job at the university, life was easier for the Curies. However, happiness wouldn't last long. In 1906, Pierre suddenly died. He was run over by a horse-drawn vehicle when he fell onto the street. He died immediately (*Pierre Curie—death*, 2014).

The death of her husband was a hard blow to Marie, but it didn't discourage her. She continued with her academic work and research at the university. After Pierre's death, she was appointed to take his place at the vacant chair, becoming the first woman to teach at the Sorbonne.

In 1910, Marie published a treatise on radioactivity, proposing a method to isolate radium. That earned her a second Nobel Prize, this time in chemistry. She is the only woman and the only scientist to have achieved a major award in science in two different fields. Sorbonne opened the first radium institute (*Institut du Radium*) under Marie's direction and started biological research to use the element in the cure of cancer and other medical applications.

Marie Curie made another contribution to science and medicine that is still used in the present. She used radium to improve X-ray machines. In 1895, Wilhelm Roentgen discovered a form of electromagnetic radiation unknown until then, which he then called X-rays. These rays could create pictures of the inside of the body. Marie Curie studied these discoveries, and in 1914, when World War I broke out, she created a small mobile X-ray machine that could be taken to the front lines.

As a member of the Red Cross, she raised funds and had the machines installed in stations near the frontlines. There, Marie and her daughter Irene used the X-ray machines called "Petits Curies" to help wounded soldiers receive a diagnosis. Bullets, fractures, and shrapnel remains could be easily located inside the body. Because of this, Marie and Irène helped save hundreds of lives.

After the end of the war, Marie was invited to be a member of the International Commission on Intellectual Cooperation of the League of Nations. She continued with her lectures and research and received awards and recognition from the most prestigious universities in the world. She presided over the opening of the Curie Foundation in Paris and the Radium Institute in Warsaw.

In the 1920s, Marie's health quickly deteriorated. She had leukemia, probably as a consequence of the extended and direct exposition to radium. She didn't know then the extremely poisonous nature of the element, and she had spent over 20 years of her life working with it and was exposed to radiation without protection (Caballero, 2016). While working in her laboratory, she used to carry tubes with radium in her pockets. She died on July 4, 1934.

The Curie's daughter, Irène, who had been with her mother on the battlefield in World War I, continued their job with her husband, Frédéric Joliot, and together won the Nobel Prize in chemistry in 1935.

Pierre and Marie Curie made a great contribution to the development of science, reducing the scope of uncertainty: They gave names to two of the elements that form what exists in the universe. They were also an example of perseverance and commitment. Marie's legacy reaches even further as her name has become a symbol of women in science, an inspiration for women all over the world.

Einstein and Mileva (1900s)

Even beyond the world of physics or science, Albert Einstein's name and face are among the most well-known people in the world. Perhaps most of them wouldn't be able to explain the theory of relativity or would mistakenly associate him with the creation of the atomic bomb, but everybody certainly knows he was one of the men who changed the world and the path of science. What most people don't know, by the way, is that he didn't work alone.

Albert Einstein's life was framed by a turbulent political environment. He was born in a little town in Germany called Ulm, in the province of Württemberg, on March 14, 1879, just a few years after the unification of the country. He lived his early years during the Second Reich, the German participation in World War I, and the Weimar Republic. He would also witness the rise of Nazism and experienced firsthand the racist persecution since he belonged to a Jewish family.

The family moved to Munich soon after Albert was born and later to Italy, but Albert went to Zurich to continue his studies. Even though he was an excellent student of math and physics, he had some trouble with other subjects, such as philosophy and history. When he was 16, he dropped out of school. However, he was later admitted to the Swiss Federal Polytechnic School and obtained a degree as a teacher but struggled to find a position. Instead, he found a job as a technical assistant at the Swiss Patent Office.

This position had nothing to do with science but gave Albert enough free time to dedicate to his own study and research. In 1905, he obtained a doctor's degree in physics. Some years later, he became a professor at Zurich and Prague and was invited to take a chair at the University of Berlin in 1914. There, he became a German citizen again until 1933, when he had to flee. By then, Hitler and the Nazi party had seized power, and his life was in danger. Albert Einstein escaped to the United States, where he thought his discoveries wouldn't fall into the wrong hands.

Albert Einstein developed the theory of general relativity and published his ideas in 1915. This theory revolutionized physics since it rejected Newton's principles that had ruled physics for 200 years. The theory of relativity could explain the movement of the planets and the existence of black holes in the universe. At first, the scientific community didn't credit Einstein for his discoveries. Many of them resisted admitting that a young professor could dethrone Newtonian physics. It wasn't until 1918 that the theory of relativity was proved by a practical experiment, and Einstein was taken seriously.

As the saying goes, behind a great man, there is always a great woman. Albert Einstein is no exception to the rule. Every time a man achieves a successful professional career, there is probably a woman taking care of trivial but not less important daily affairs that allow the man to focus on his career. Einstein had a woman by his side to support him and assist him in the early years of his career when he didn't have an important position as a physicist and wasn't a renowned scientist.

Her name was Mileva Marić, and she was Albert Einstein's first wife. She is less known than his second wife, who accompanied him during his years in the United States when he was already a popular man and visiting governments and prestigious academic institutions. Mileva was beside Einstein in his difficult years when he was a young man making his way into the world, trying to make the world listen to his ideas.

Nonetheless, Mileva wasn't only a devoted wife and housekeeper in charge of domestic affairs, she was also concerned about physics and science as well, and an example of the relegated role of women from the academic world in the early 20th century.

Mileva was born in 1875 in Titel, Serbia, but at that time, it was part of the Austro-Hungarian Empire. As a child, she attended school in Zagreb, and all her classmates were boys. The same happened when she entered the Swiss Federal Polytechnic School. There were five students, and she was the only girl. One of the four boys was Albert Einstein.

Since she was a child, Mileva proved an excellent disposition to learn mathematics and physics. It is believed she even surpassed Albert's genius. Nonetheless, Mileva didn't graduate due to her professor's unjust way of conducting the final exams. As classmates, they became inseparable, even after Albert achieved the degree and Mileva couldn't. They got married in Bern, Switzerland, in 1903.

Despite this, Albert was aware of the brilliance of Mileva's mind and carried out all his research to develop the theory of relativity with her help. It was a difficult time for the couple, but they shared their passion for science. The first version of the theory, written in 1905, was a result of the cooperation of the couple. Nonetheless, only Albert's name was given as the author of the paper. It is believed that the Einstein family didn't approve of the marriage. They didn't want their son linked to a Serbian who was older than him (Carlton, 2022). The opposition of his family prevented Albert from sharing his accomplishments with his wife, even though most of it was her own work.

While Albert worked at the patent office, he didn't only develop the first ideas to propose the theory of general relativity, his contributions to quantum and atomic theory were also developed at that time. His most famous formula, $E = mc^2$, was introduced while he worked a low-income job to support the family and his personal research. Meanwhile, Mileva supported him and gave birth to their two children, Hans Albert and Eduard.

All that time, when Albert struggled to find a place within the select intellectual environment of Europe, Mileva was at his side. Thanks to the intense correspondence Albert had with his wife, which was published in 1969, the world now knows the important role she played in Einstein's life. In the letters, many scholars argue to find clear evidence of the significant contributions made by Mileva to Einstein in helping him to develop his theories (Esterson & Cassidy, 2019).

However, the marriage wouldn't last long. Just a few years after Einstein found a good position as a professor, he decided to divorce his wife. In 1914, he proposed a compromise to continue the marriage to keep appearances but under new conditions. According to the statement, the money of the Nobel Prize, if he won it, would be given to her. It is interesting to wonder why Einstein would do such a thing.

When he eventually won the Nobel Prize in physics in 1921, he tried to take his promise back, but Mileva claimed she had enough evidence to prove she was the one to be credited for many of Einstein's contributions to science. Somehow, Einstein chose to keep his promise, but he wrote to his ex-wife in a letter: "When someone is completely insignificant, there is nothing else to say to this person but to remain modest and silent. This is what I advise you to do" (Carlton, 2022).

The couple finally got divorced in 1919, and in 1922, Mileva received the prize money, which is equivalent to about $500,000 today. Nonetheless, that was barely enough for her to keep up with her two children. She couldn't afford a professional career. Instead, she dedicated herself to taking care of her sons, especially Eduard, who had been diagnosed with schizophrenia. Mileva died in 1948, and Eduard was placed in a hospice. His father didn't see him for the last 30 years. Mileva and Albert's oldest son moved with his family to the United States.

Albert Einstein was considered "the man of the century," and his theories still frame the contemporary view of the universe. Most of his contributions have been used in thousands of further discoveries and technological developments, including nuclear energy and GPS. On the other hand, Mileva's name remains in the shadows. Her role in Einstein's life is underestimated, and her contributions to his ultimate theories are questioned or denied. Even if she didn't help Einstein achieve his revolutionary theory, she still deserves to be credited for postponing her personal interests and professional career to boost her husband.

Jean-Paul Sartre and Simone de Beauvoir (1900s)

The 1960s were years of revolution, particularly in Europe. The world, after the end of the Second World War, dreamed of a new era for humankind. The youth hoisted the flags of imagination instead of reason and claimed peace to tear down the Iron Curtain. In France, in May 1968, hundreds of longed-haired boys and girls with short skirts raised their voices against the status quo, the war in Vietnam, and the unwieldy structures of the bourgeoisie. Among those young boys and girls, two of them had joined their lives and brought together their ideas to create a new paradigm for a brand-new world. Their names were Jean-Paul Sartre and Simone de Beauvoir. He was later known as the father of existentialism and Simone, the forerunner of the second wave of feminism.

He was born on June 21, 1905, in Paris. He was a renowned philosopher, writer, and playwright who used his novels and plays to expose his ideas. Most of what is known from his life was told by himself in his famous autobiography titled *Les Mots* (*The Words* in English, written in 1963. Jean-Paul lost his father when he was a child, and despite having the most refined education in prestigious institutions, he was a lonely child who felt he didn't fit anywhere. Eventually, his books and his writing were how he escaped the world. At least, that is how he pictured himself in *Les Mots*.

He graduated from the École Normale Supérieure in 1929 and became a professor at the lycées of Le Havre, Laon, and, finally, Paris. He taught there between 1931 and 1945. During his life as a student and professor, he had the opportunity to meet the greatest minds of his time. He had the chance to study phenomenology under the direction of its precursors, Husserl and Heidegger, who invited Sartre to spend a year in Germany. In France, Jean-Paul shared the select intellectual circle with great names such as Raymond Aron, Simone Weil, and Claude Lévi-Strauss (Desan, 2023).

His intellectual activity halted in 1939 when he was forced to fight on the front during World War II. He had published one of his most famous books, *La Nausée* (*Nausea* in English). While in combat, Jean-Paul was taken prisoner and kept incarcerated for a year. He was released in 1940. The war left a deep impression on Jean-Paul and led his attention toward social responsibility. He engaged in active political movements linked to left-wing ideas, although he never joined the French Communist Party.

When the social uprising started in Paris in May 1968, he joined the students who had taken the Sorbonne. But then, Jean-Paul wasn't alone. His partner in life was with him. She was Simone de Beauvoir.

They had met in 1929 while they were both studying at the École Normale Supérieure. Like him, Simone rejected the social stereotypes and the corset that the rules of "bourgeois marriage" (as they called it) set to love. Instead, they fell in love and started a long-lasting relationship based on freedom and non-exclusivity, where the only requirement was total honesty. However, Simone and Jean-Paul shared much more than an innovative romantic relationship. Together, they collaborated to create a disruptive thinking movement.

Simone's full name was Simone-Lucie-Ernestine-Marie Bertrand de Beauvoir, and she was born on January 9, 1908, in Paris. She came from a wealthy bourgeois family, but she always resisted the traditional way of life. It is believed that her early renouncement of Catholicism and rejection of marriage persuaded Jean-Paul to accept a relationship under their own rules. As classmates at the École and also the Sorbonne, they studied together to be an aggregate in philosophy. Jean-Paul achieved better marks than Simone, but she became the youngest person to pass the exam. She was only 21 (Encyclopaedia Britannica, 2023c).

She didn't think of herself as a philosopher, although she shared with her partner all her intellectual activity. Instead, she considered herself a writer and admitted to a strong influence of Sartré on her work. She expressed existentialism through the stories told in her books. At the same time, Sartré always mentioned the mutual influence between the two of them. They shared their life and work without ever living in the same house. They would meet at the university, parks, and cafes to discuss their ideas and write.

Jean-Paul and Simone were together for 51 years. During those years, each of them wrote and published important works considered the foundations of existentialism and the second wave of feminism. Both of them were writers in the first place.

Sartre spent the first years of his career writing philosophy and novels and later dedicated himself to writing plays. *La Nausée* was published in 1938, but most of his famous works were published after the war. *L'Être et le néant (Being and Nothingness*, 1943) and *L'Existentialisme est un humanisme (Existencialism and Humanism*, 1946) are two of his best remembered treatises on philosophy and are considered the foundations of existentialism. Later, his plays and collaborations with the playwright Albert Camus set a landmark for existentialism and the theater of the absurd. They expressed that the human being didn't actually have a purpose in life, and its ideal can be summarized in Sartre's statement, "existence precedes essence," the subversion of the traditional cartesian rule "I think, therefore I am." Sartre's existentialism is centered on the human being and his capacity to be free, though not in a liberal way, but committed to social responsibility.

Jean-Paul Sartre was a man of strong convictions and lived his life with coherence. In 1964, he was awarded the Nobel Prize in Literature, but he refused to accept it. He wrote a letter to the Royal Swedish Academy of Sciences to decline the award, arguing that culture and arts shouldn't be restrained by institutions and normative systems. Framed by the Cold War, Sartre believed that accepting the prize would place him in one of both contestant sides.

Simone de Beauvoir was never nominated for the Nobel Prize but received many other international awards. Her work doesn't lack recognition beyond her link with Sartre. Her treatise *Le Deuxième Sexe*, 2 vol (translated as *The Second Sex* in English), published in 1949, is the main reference book of the feminist second wave in the 20th century. The first wave of the feminist movement was carried out by the suffragette movement. This was the fight of women to achieve political rights during the 19th century and the first decades of the 20th century. de Beauvoir represents a fight that goes further, denouncing that the capitalist system entails a patriarchal society that relegates women to a second place. Women are forced to assume social roles subordinated to men's power.

All of Simone's work claimed the abolition of the myth of the eternal feminine. As she said, one is not born a woman but becomes one (Dead Wild Roses, 2019). It is society and its rules that impose on women gender traits that limit their chances to decide what and how they want to be and restrain their access to power and participation. Even though Simone is considered a pioneer of 20th-century feminism, she didn't join the French Feminine Movement until 20 years later after publishing *The Second Sex*. She believed the liberation of women and equality would be achieved through a socialist revolution. The situation of women in socialist regimes proved to her that it was unlikely to happen (Meisler, 1986).

Besides their prolific life as writers that both of them had, they also engaged in common projects, especially regarding social participation and the expression of a political position. Jean-Paul and Simone founded and edited a monthly review called *Le Temps Modernes*. The first edition was published in 1945 and endured for 70 years. The main referents of all the intellectual production appeared on its pages, including remarkable names such as Lacan, Bourdieu, Foucault, and Habermas, who chose the magazine to spread their theories. Jean-Paul and Simone also joined a clandestine activist group called "Socialisme et Liberté" in the 1940s. When the social turmoil arose in Paris in 1968, the couple stood up for the students who took the University of the

Sorbonne and the streets of Paris. One of the main mottos was "Soyez réalistes, demandez l'impossible," which translates to "Be realistic, ask the impossible" (Del Campo, 2019).

Jean-Paul Sartre stopped his intellectual activity in the 1970s when he became blind, and his health quickly deteriorated. He died in April 1980. Then, the woman who had been by his side all his life wrote: "His death does separate us. My death will not bring us together again. That is how things are" (Meisler, 1986, para. 5). She survived him for six years and died in Paris on April 14, 1986. He will always be remembered for his belief in human beings' freedom and relentless search for truth. She will always be the main founder of the contemporary feminist movement committed to breaking the chains that subjugate women. Together, they represent the ideals of a generation that tried to change the world.

Chapter 2:

Activist Duos

Elizabeth Cady Stanton and Susan B. Anthony (1800s)

The 19th century witnessed unprecedented technological advances and political evolution. The capitalist system strengthened at the time the market spread, and the Industrial Revolution expanded the limits of wealth. Scientific development nurtured the ideal of endless progress for humankind. In America, people fought for their freedom, and new states emerged after breaking the colonial bonds with the old European Empire. Nonetheless, the blessings of changes didn't reach all the social groups equally. Even in the new land of freedom, slaves, workers, and women had to struggle to survive and open their paths in an unjust society. In the United States, two women embraced the ideals of justice and equality and led the fight for the rights of the unprivileged. Their names were Elizabeth and Susan.

Elizabeth Cady was born in Johnstown, New York on November 12, 1815. As the daughter of a member of the House of Representatives of the United States and later a New York Supreme Court judge, Elizabeth had the opportunity to study law, a not-so-common prerogative for women at that time. In fact, she had been banned from the university simply for being a woman. Later, she was able to study at her father's office. She graduated in 1832 from Johnstown Academy. During her years as a student, she learned the many legal conditions that restrained women's rights in the country. So, she decided she would fight to change that.

In 1840, Elizabeth got married to Henry Brewster Stanton. He was a lawyer who advocated for the abolition of slavery. The same year as their wedding, Elizabeth accompanied her husband to a summit in London to attend the World's Anti-Slavery Convention. There, she and Lucretia Mott, a Quaker minister from Pennsylvania, were denied participation. That episode triggered Elizabeth's determination to take action.

Back in the United States, she became a speaker on human rights and passed a petition to the New York legislature claiming married women's property rights. However, Elizabeth Stanton would do much more than simply speak. Elizabeth and Lucretia wouldn't easily forget they had been banned for being women and decided that if a world made for males wouldn't let them participate, they would build a space on their own. In a tea party hosted by Jane Hunt, Lucretia Mott, Elizabeth Cady, and other neighboring women of Seneca Falls decided to organize a convention "to discuss the social, civil, and religious condition of women" (*The Declaration of Sentiments*, 2023). It would be the first convention for women's rights, and it took place on July 19th and 20th of 1848, in Seneca Falls, where Elizabeth lived. At that time, the movement for workers' rights had arisen in Europe, and the abolition of slavery was discussed in the United States, but women's rights weren't yet on the main political agenda. Elizabeth then became a pioneer in the fight for women's rights.

To promote the convention, Elizabeth wrote a protest statement called *A Declaration of Sentiments*. It was a sharp critic of the legislation of the Republican system that conceded property privileges to men over women. She covered all inequalities that hampered women's participation in public affairs: social class, ethnical, and regional differences (*The Declaration of Sentiments*, 2023).

At the summit, Elizabeth met a woman who soon became a dear friend and a camaraderie in her campaign. Her name was Susan Brownell Anthony, and she was from Adams, Massachusetts. She was born on February 15, 1820. When they met, both women were in their 30s and would remain together in their fight for the rest of their lives despite some differences they found on their way.

Susan was born to a family ruled by the Quaker tradition. Her mother belonged to a family that had been part of the American Revolution. Under her mother's influence and her father's thoughts about all people being equal in front of God, Susan became an advocate for the abolition of slavery and equal rights for everybody since she was very young. She was a witty girl who learned to read and write when she was only 3 and later received a devoted education at the school opened by her father near Philadelphia. Then, she became a teacher, first at the Quaker seminary in Rochelle and in academia in New York.

While teaching in New York, she met many other women engaged in the abolitionist struggle. Among them, Susan met Amelia Bloomer, a writer and activist who invited her to attend the Seneca Falls convention three years after the first national women's rights convention. On that occasion, in 1851, Amelia introduced Susan to Elizabeth on a street corner. From then on, they became inseparable. Each of them assumed a role to empower the other and together foster the suffrage movement in America. It would be a long and tough path to walk along.

Susan was an active participant in social movements and wanted to contribute to creating a better society. She took part in the temperance movement, which promoted moderation of alcohol consumption. This movement, founded in New York, was mainly coordinated by the churches. In 1852, Susan wanted to speak during the assembly carried out in Albany, but she was rejected. Therefore, she decided to organize a movement on her own. She founded the Woman's New York State Temperance Society. By then, Elizabeth and Susan had joined forces to fight together. Susan asked her friend to be the president of the organization, and Elizabeth accepted but redirected the fight to advocate for women's rights.

Their main claims were regarding women's rights within marriage, for instance, the liberalization of divorce laws that enabled women to dissolve a marriage when they found it inconvenient and the wives' rights on the properties. They also supported women's freedom to dress as they wished without any specific regulation. They advocated for equal opportunities for women to access health, education, and work opportunities. Later, Susan and Elizabeth would focus on political rights and represented in America the suffrage movement that had gained force in Europe in the last decades of the 19th century.

Beyond advocating for women's rights, Susan and Elizabeth engaged in all the current social changes. During the Civil War, they joined the abolitionists and founded the Women's National Loyal League. They gathered over 300 thousand signatures to support the petition for complete enfranchisement of African American people after the war and, later, equal right to vote for African men and women. They were greatly disappointed when men were effectively afforded that right, but women were still excluded.

Far from giving up, both women redoubled their efforts to reach the amendment included in the constitution to ensure equal political rights for women. In 1868, Elizabeth, in association with Parker Pillsbury, became the editor of the weekly newspaper called *The Revolution*. She was also the president of the National Woman Suffrage Association and wrote the Declaration of Rights for Women and the amendment introduced by the U.S. Congress until it was definitely included in the Constitution in 1920.

However, Elizabeth and Susan's struggle wasn't limited to writing and speaking. In 1872, Susan cast a vote in the presidential election in Rochester, New York. For that action, she was arrested and was found guilty. Her sentence was written before the trial, and she denounced the fraud of an illegitimate procedure. She was given a fine of $100, but she refused to pay as it would be a way to admit a crime she didn't believe to have committed and was eventually released. Her detention motivated demonstrations in different states, and the suffrage movement called the attention of the national government.

Elizabeth and Susan also wrote together the first three volumes of the *History of Woman Suffrage*, a book that gathers speeches, correspondence, and other manuscripts that document the evolution of the suffrage movement in the United States. They traveled across all the states, giving speeches and inspiring other women to stand up for their rights. While Elizabeth wrote most of the documents and speeches, Susan was in charge of the strategy to organize the movement and the meetings. Together, they were unstoppable.

At the beginning of the 20th century, both women continued with their untiring fight, although time and health issues forced them to be separated. Nonetheless, they continued working together, sharing ideas and strength through intense correspondence.

Elizabeth died in 1902, and Susan died at the age of 86, four years later. They couldn't see the outcome of their struggle come true. Despite all their efforts, women still had to fight for almost another 20 years before achieving the right to vote in 1920. It is undeniable that Elizabeth and Susan steered the course for the suffrage movement and pioneered the feminist vindications regarding a fairer place for women within society.

Helen Keller and Anne Sullivan (1900s)

Living with any disability can be discouraging for most people. Even at present, with all the medical advances and the technological devices that can make things a little bit easier, it is hard to be disabled in a world made for able-bodied people. It isn't too difficult to imagine how much harder it must have been 100 years ago. Despite the great challenges that being disabled encompassed, the self-determination of a young girl and the love, patience, and devotion of her teacher and friend proved to everybody there are no limits to overcoming the odds.

Helen Keller was born on June 27, 1880, in Tuscumbia, a little town in Alabama. When she was only 19 months old, Helen was afflicted by a terrible illness. It could have been rubella or scarlet fever. While these illnesses aren't so dangerous now, at the time, there were very few medical procedures to treat them. So, in the 19th century, it left irreversible damage to those afflicted, and Helen became deaf and blind.

She grew up without being able to express herself and without the chance to play and learn like any other child. She became a rebellious child who couldn't be controlled by her parents, Kate and Arthur. She would have outrageous tantrums that no one could control and would mistreat all the people around her. She was growing up alone and probably felt very sad, frustrated, and lonely because of that. Helen was a very clever child, but nobody could find a way to reach out to her.

When she was 6 years old, Doctor Alexander Graham Bell examined her and advised her parents to find her a teacher, someone who could spend time with her to show the world around her. Soon, Helen's life would change forever when Anne came to her house to be her tutor.

Anne's name was Joanna Sullivan, and she came from Massachusetts. She was 20 years old when she met the girl who would be her only pupil, Helen. She was only 14 years older than her student.

Perhaps because she had had a difficult life herself, Anne approached the rebellious child with compassion. Anne came from a poor family of Irish immigrants and lost her mother when she was 8. Anne and her siblings were abandoned by her father two years later. She was in the custody of the state of Massachusetts and spent four terrible years in an orphanage. Eventually, Anne entered the Perkins School, an institution for the blind, as she had serious vision problems herself. She had a bacterial infection in her eyes when she was 5, and she was partially sighted. Therefore, Anne could perfectly understand how Helen felt.

Unlike Helen, Anne could have part of her vision restored. After a year at Perkins, she had surgery that established some sight. Two years later, she graduated as a teacher. She dedicated several months to studying how to teach the blind and students with special needs. Anne followed the works conducted by Samuel Gridley Howe, founder of Perkins School for the Blind, where she had formed herself as a teacher. She was deeply moved by Laura Dewey Bridgman's story, a deaf and blind woman who developed the ability to communicate by using finger spelling to write words. Laura was able to hold a conversation and even speak in public. Anne had acquired the resources to teach but was also persuaded that a better life was possible for people with disabilities.

Being a resilient person herself, Anne landed at the Keller's to be the governess of little Helen. The relationship between the little girl and her teacher didn't go well from the beginning. Helen continued with her temper tantrums, but soon, Anne found a way to calm down the child. Within a month, Anne and Helen had made impressive progress not only in their bond but in all the things the child learned.

Anne had spent a lot of time with Laura during her time at Perkins and had learned from her the methods to communicate. So, she tried to implement them to teach Helen. The teacher kindly took her student's hand and drew the letters with her finger on the palm of the little hand. She would draw letter by letter, spelling a word so the child could associate it with the object. It wasn't easy.

The first word Anne tried was "doll." She drew the shape of the letters in Helen's hand and then put the toy in her hand. Even though Helen could repeat the letters, she couldn't understand what the word meant. When Anne changed the toy, Helen would still spell "doll." It was another word that made the difference. That was the word "water" (Sartore, 2021).

Anne spelled W-A-T-E-R in Helen's hand and immediately put the same hand into the water. Then, Helen could link the letters with the thing. It was a turning point in her education. Anne's patience and creativity were bearing fruit. Within a few weeks, Helen learned over 100 words (Sartore, 2021). She would touch here and there and ask Anne to spell the words with her fingers. Helen repeated the letters until she learned the word, and slowly, she could name the world around her.

But that wasn't all Anne could teach Helen. The girl was brilliant and had an unlimited curiosity and thirst to learn. So, the young teacher started with lessons in other subjects like arithmetic and botany. Then, she took Helen to Perkins to meet other girls and soon started with vocal training. Within some time, Helen could also speak.

Helen and Anne's educational experience was soon known outside the city and the state, in part thanks to Alexander Graham Bell, who spoke about them in an article published in the newspaper. Anne encouraged Helen's parents to let her experience the world, and the visits to Perkins were just the beginning of many trips they took together. They started visiting cities and institutions to talk about their experience. In 1887, they were invited to the opening of the Volta Bureau for deaf research, and in 1888, they met President Cleveland. A few years later, Helen and Anne met the famous writer Mark Twain, who was deeply impressed by the girl's development and by her teacher's talent. The writer asked his own benefactor, Henry Rogers of Standard Oil, to help

Helen. With Rogers' financial assistance, Helen could continue her studies after graduating from Perkins (Hare, 2015).

Anne accompanied Helen throughout all of her life, even after getting married and despite her weak health. In 1914, Helen hired a new assistant since Anne was already affected by her health problems. Anne died in 1936, and even though Helen had a new assistant, she never forgot the friend and teacher who transformed her world.

Besides the personal journey of self-overcoming, Helen and Anne shared many other accomplishments with a great impact on their community and posterity. Helen learned to communicate in Braille and to speak, but she also achieved many other educational goals. She was the first Deafblind person to graduate from Radcliffe College (present-day Harvard University) and advocate for better opportunities for blind people as a member of the American Foundation for the Blind. Furthermore, she joined and supported other organizations that promoted workers' and women's rights (Waxman, 2020). She became a writer and wrote for women's magazines and published several books, including her autobiography entitled *The Story of My Life*. Helen's life is better known in the world for her incredible story of overcoming disabilities as a child, but her achievements in adulthood were also very important and inspiring. She didn't only share her life as an example and taught her method but also engaged in social activism.

Helen Keller and Anne Sullivan are considered pioneers and inspirers of the changes in the educational system to promote and ensure inclusive education.

Gandhi and Jawaharlal Nehru (1900s)

The history of humankind hasn't only been shaped by Western culture. Political and social processes that took place in distant corners of the globe have contributed to creating the present. Struggles for freedom and justice have helped develop a global community where everybody's rights matter. It was a fight that took centuries and was led by people of all ethnicities. For many years, some continents evolved under the yoke of imperialism, but people never gave up on their true identity and desire for liberty. This is the story of two men who fought for the independence of their country but spread a message of peace and justice for all. Mohandas Gandhi and Jawaharlal Nehru led the nonviolent political movement in India and became a symbol of the decolonization process.

His name was Mohandas Karamchand Gandhi, but everybody remembers him as Mahatma, which means "Great Soul." He was born on October 2, 1869 in Porbandar. At that time, his country was under the political rule of the British Empire, and the Indian population was organized in a caste system. According to the caste they belonged to, people were deprived of a number of rights. Only a few belonged to the privileged caste, while most of the population lived in poverty.

Mohandas belonged to the Vaisia caste, a segment with certain privileges. His father was the dewan (the chief minister) of Porbandar, which was the capital city of a small principality. Therefore, Mohandas rose in a family with a bit of power. His mother, Putlibai, was a very devoted woman who spent most of her time at the temple. The Gandhis believed in the Hindi god Vishnu and followed the Jainism morals. This taught Mohandas to avoid any action that could hurt other beings. From his early stages, he observed nonviolence as a way of living, as well as vegetarianism and fasting to purify the body and soul.

When he was 19 years old, he was sent to England like many boys from the higher castes in India. During his stay in England, he entered the Inner Temple to study law. The people he met introduced him to some of the most prominent names of Western culture. Mohandas became interested in learning about other cultures and religions. After achieving an academic degree, he decided to go back to his country instead of entering the Court of London.

In 1891, back in India, he tried to work as a lawyer, but life had changed too much for him in his birthland. His father had died while he was still at school, and his mother had died in his absence as well. Without a plan in India, he joined a businessman who took him to South Africa. When he was in the African country, Mohandas lived an experience that marked him forever.

He was traveling on a train to Pretoria in a first-class seat. Then, a White person who had to sit in the same wagon complained to the White police about the train because there was an Indian person in it. In South Africa at that time, people were still divided by the color of their skin and their ethnicity. That determined what rights they had or lacked. The coolies (the way Indians were called) didn't have the right to be in the same wagon as the White people. Gandhi was told to leave his seat, and as he refused, the police pushed him off the train. He was humiliated, but he didn't fight against it.

While in South Africa, Mohandas became a leader who advocated for the rights of the Indian minority in the country. He was a former member of the Natal Indian Congress (NIC), and it was there where he used for the first time the *satyagraha*. This was a passive way to protest that meant "truth force." Mohandas said that oppression only existed if both subjects agreed on that. If the oppressed could see the truth beyond that bond, then they would be free (*Mohandas Karamchand Gandhi*, n.d.).

Gandhi started his fight against the British colonial occupation in South Africa but went back to India. He arrived in Bombay in 1915, almost a year after the outbreak of World War I. There, he became almost immediately involved in the Indian National Congress: The Congress Party. In the annual meeting that year, he met the man who would become the first prime minister of free India.

Jawaharlal Nehru was born on November 14, 1889, in Allahabad, India. He belonged to a family of Kashmiri Brahmans, and his father was engaged in the Indian independence cause. He completed the first part of his education at home with tutors who instructed him in English and sciences. When he was 16, he went to Cambridge to study law. After achieving his degree, he went back to India as a lawyer. There, he got married and tried to establish himself as a lawyer, but with little success.

The end of World War I opened a new scenario for the Indians' nationalist vindications. Nehru, like most young men of his time, wanted to fight for the freedom of his country but didn't know how. He eventually joined the Congress Party, the organization that led the action against the British. The years that followed the end of the war were of increasing violence in India. People gathered in the streets to demonstrate against the British Empire, and the army opened fire against the crowd, killing hundreds of people. Nehru and other demonstrators were imprisoned several times. Jawaharlal spent nine years total, counting all the times he was arrested between 1919 when the uprising began, and 1945, when the process of independence was finally geared.

In the 1920s, under the strong leadership of Mohandas Gandhi, the political figure of Nehru began to grow. Together, they turned the Congress Party into an effective instrument of independence. They organized massive demonstrations in the most important cities of the country, gathering people from the small towns and villages. Despite the violent repression of the government, Gandhi and his partner proposed a nonviolent and noncooperation movement. They wouldn't use weapons or confront the police but use boycotts as a measure of strength. They used satyagraha as a means to fight.

The Indians would boycott not only English goods and companies but also all their institutions and laws. It was peaceful civil disobedience, a form of passive resistance. Thousands of satyagrahis were imprisoned, including Gandhi and Nehru. The massive movement turned violent on many occasions as they couldn't manage the multitudes. Nonetheless, in 1924, Mohandas Gandhi assumed a three-week fast to call people to continue their struggle by the nonviolent path. He succeeded.

The Congress Party was consolidated, and Nehru and Gandhi were its indisputable leaders. During the 1930s, the Congress and the British government started negotiations to accept the independence of India. Nonetheless, the outbreak of World War II put a halt to negotiations. In the beginning, the Congress offered support to the British forces if the autonomous Indian government was ensured, but when the fight against the Axis powers intensified, the British government took prisoner all the Congress authorities, including Gandhi and Nehru. They were kept in the Aga Khan Palace (Nanda, 2023).

After World War II ended, the Labour Party won in Great Britain, negotiations reopened, and independence was finally achieved. However, the final result was nothing like what Gandhi and Nehru had imagined. The country was divided into India and Pakistan, and the conflicts due to religious differences between Muslims and Hindus continued for decades.

Jawaharlal Nehru was elected Prime Minister. He represented the secular face of the Congress Party and Indian nationalism. His political leadership strengthened when, in 1929, Gandhi chose him as his successor as the president of the party. From then on, he became the political leader of the movement. On the other hand, Gandhi represented the traditional values of the Indian people and the spiritual side of the movement. Together, they found a way to represent the deep interests of the Indian community in times of social turmoil, uncertainty, and chaos. They spoke about freedom and peace while the world passed through two terrible world wars. They left a message of peaceful resistance and an unwavering fight for justice and equal rights for every person, regardless of the color of their skin or their religious beliefs.

Martin Luther King Jr. and Ralph Abernathy Sr. (1900s)

Despite the horrors of war and the increasing concern in the world for ensuring human rights, in many countries, people lacked several prerogatives for their ethnic origins. In the United States, almost a century after the abolition of slavery, Black people were still treated like second-class citizens. It wasn't only social prejudice and discrimination, it was a legal system enacted to establish certain prohibitions for Black people, places where they couldn't be, and roles in society they couldn't play. In the 1950s and 1960s, Black people broke their silence and started fighting to be treated for what they were: equal citizens of the United States and human beings who deserved the same rights and respect as White people. Martin Luther King and Ralph Abernathy were two of the most representative leaders of the Civil Rights Movement.

His name at birth was Michael King, and he was born on January 15, 1929, in Atlanta, Georgia. His father and his grandfather were both Baptist preachers, and that had a great influence on Michael. He grew up in a wealthy middle-class family that lived on the street where the most prosperous Black people's businesses were located. Even though he didn't suffer economic shortages and had access to a good education, Michael wasn't ignorant of the needs of most Black people in his country, particularly in the South where he lived.

When he was 6 years old, Michael experienced the pain of being discriminated against. His friends, who were from White families, told him they weren't allowed to play with him anymore. They would start attending a segregated school where Black and White children didn't share classrooms or playgrounds. Little Michael was heartbroken.

In 1944, Michael went to Connecticut to work on a tobacco farm. There, he was surprised to find that in the North, White and Black people coexisted peacefully, and there was no segregation due to racial bias. That made Michael determined to go back home and fight against racial segregation.

Despite the chances he had to study medicine or law, Michael had decided to become a minister. He had heard the message of the social activist Benjamin Mays, who claimed that the Black church should be an instrument of their people's struggle for justice and equality. Michael decided to follow his steps. He studied at Morehouse and graduated in 1948, but he then spent another three years at the Crozer Theological Seminary in Chester, Pennsylvania. As a student, he excelled for his impressive skills as a speaker. That was how Ralph Abernathy met him.

Ralph was born on March 11, 1926, in Linden, Alabama. His father was the son of a slave who had managed to own a farm and thrive. Young Ralph helped his father with the business while he attended the Baptist church to serve as a deacon. When he grew up, he studied at the University of Alabama. He was interested in sociology and math, but he eventually decided to become a minister. After serving as a soldier overseas during World War II, he was ordained as a Baptist minister in 1948.

He was still a student when he first heard a heated speech given by Michael from the pulpit of the Ebenezer Baptist Church. Ralph was deeply moved by Michael's words, and after the ceremony, he introduced himself to the minister. It was the beginning of an enduring friendship based on a common purpose: the achievement of equal civil rights for every citizen.

Ralph and Michael organized one of the most important landmarks in the struggle for Black people's civil rights. On December 1st, 1955, a Black woman named Rosa Parks was sitting on a bus in Montgomery. By then, buses had a line that divided the seats reserved for White people. The Black had to sit at the back of the bus. That day, the bus was full, and White people continued to get on the bus. At one point, there were no free seats on the White's side. Rosa was sitting in the first row on the Black's side. The bus driver approached her and ordered her to leave the seat so White people could take it, but Rosa didn't move. She was eventually pushed off the bus and arrested for rejecting the segregation law.

Martin Luther King and Ralph Abernathy, who was, by then, pastor of Montgomery's First Baptist Church, thought it was the moment to act. Both of them were greatly influenced by Gandhi's nonviolent philosophy and also proposed a peaceful means to protest. They chose a method used by the Indians fighting for their freedom under Gandhi and Nehru's leadership: boycott. Baptist ministers were the leaders of the Montgomery Improvement Association and called on Black people of their community not to use public means of transport.

For more than a year, Black people would walk to work and school or would eventually take a cab, but they wouldn't take the bus. The level of adherence to the protest was high and enduring. There were many attempts to try and make them decline their position. Martin Luther King's house was dynamited, and something similar happened to Abernathy's house and church, but neither of them stepped back. On the contrary, they held the boycott until, in 1957, the buses were eventually desegregated.

In 1957, Abernathy and King joined other African leaders to form the Southern Christian Leadership Conference (SCLC), an organization that attempted to spread the movement across the country. Martin

Luther King decided to move back to his birth state, Atlanta, to lead the movement in the South. Abernathy became the president of the association.

In Atlanta, King was arrested after supporting a demonstration against segregation carried out by young people in Georgia. While he was in prison, President Eisenhower intervened, although he didn't succeed in achieving freedom for the social leader. King was eventually released thanks to the mediation of the Democrat Party candidate for the presidency, John F. Kennedy. Then, Martin Luther King became a national figure. From then on, his public speeches were being covered by national media and became more and more popular.

Even though Martin Luther King became the visible face of the civil rights movement, Ralph's support was vital for his activity and the permanence of the movement. In 1960, King assigned Abernathy as the minister of the West Hunter Baptist Church in Atlanta. He accepted the position and moved to Atlanta. Then, he became the vice president of the SCLC.

Despite the strength of the movement and the achievements King and Abernathy had together, they also had many detractors. The nonviolent strategy was intensely questioned, especially after the emergence of the Black Power movement in the 1960s. Among their most relevant achievements, it is worth mentioning the Civil Rights Act passed in 1964 and the Voting Act of 1965. Martin Luther King was awarded the Nobel Peace Prize in 1964.

King and Abernathy continued their struggle for peace and the end of racial discrimination, one by carrying out the public campaign and the other by serving the organization and leading the church that had been the foundation stone of the movement. Nonetheless, on April 4, 1968, Martin Luther King was killed by a sniper while he was standing on the balcony of his motel room. He was in Memphis, Tennessee, to support a strike of sanitation workers.

After his friend's death, Abernathy became the president of the SCLC and continued with the activist plans they had started. They aimed to organize the Poor People's Campaign, and Abernathy didn't give up on his efforts to do it until he resigned his charge in 1977.

Time and history have remembered better the name of Martin Luther King Jr. and relegated Ralph Abernathy. While working together, one became the one to speak up in public while the other remained working on the basis of the movement. Both of them were indispensable to building a just and equal society. King's speeches have become words of hope and faith for humankind that have transcended generations and frontiers, but behind those words stands the silent work of Ralph Abernathy and his unselfish dedication to the human rights cause.

Chapter 3:

Explorer Duos

Hernán Cortés and La Malinche (1500s)

Historical duos presented in the previous chapters were gathered by common interests and a purpose they both aimed to achieve. The first duo of this chapter is rather atypical. They came from different worlds and had diametrical views and interests, but still, they met and built for themselves a future together. At first sight, it is hard to imagine how a Spanish conqueror and a Native American princess could find reasons to join their paths. When learning about their story, it becomes clear that there are some traits that are universal and not restrained by any cultural influence. Hernán Cortés and La Malinche were enchanted by an impossible and irrepressible attraction and the instinctive drive to survive.

After Cristopher Columbus's first arrival at the lands on the West across the ocean, the Spanish crown sent several expeditions to explore the new territories. Soon, they realized it wasn't India but a whole new continent full of wealth and powerful empires. Hernán Cortés was the first of the Spanish explorers to run into one of those empires and confront them.

About his birth, it is only known the year and area: 1485, in a village near Extremadura in the reign of Castile. He belonged to a noble family with no wealth. In an attempt to revert his luck and raise a fortune, he moved to the south of the recently unified country. At first, he thought of becoming a soldier, but while he was in the city of Valencia, he saw the ships coming from the Occidental Indias (America) with loads of goods, gold, and silver. Then, he decided he would be an explorer and make himself rich.

He boarded a Spanish ship as a member of the crew, and in 1504, he landed on the island of Hispaniola (present-day Santo Domingo) in the Caribbean Sea, where the first settlements had been established. After some time living as a farmer, he took part in the mission that conquered Cuba, and later, he led a new expedition that headed West to explore a more distant shore. It was the peninsula of Yucatan.

Hernán Cortés and 11 ships sailed to Yucatán on February 18, 1519. He had an army of about 500 men. As soon as he landed, he met the local people. Among them was a woman who was very different from the other members of her community. Cortés was fascinated with this woman not only because of her beauty but also her wit. She could communicate with foreigners and spoke several native languages. Hernán Cortés took her as his personal companion.

This woman's real name could have been Malinal or Malintzin in her native language (Encyclopaedia Britannica, 2023e; Mohammed, 2019). However, the Spanish gave her the name of Doña Marina. Instead, the Aztecs called her La Malinche. She came from a noble Aztec family. Malinche was the daughter of an Aztec cacique (king), but after her father's death, she was sold as a slave to the cacique of a tribe in Tobasco. This is where Cortés met her. Some historians believe she didn't join the Spanish voluntarily. Instead, she was a gift (Innes, 2023).

When the Native American people first saw the Europeans, they believed they were the envies of the gods. Therefore, they received them with devotion. The first encounters were peaceful, as nobody knew the other's intentions. So, they exchanged presents as proof of friendship. Slaves were common among the Native people in the Yucatan peninsula, and that is how probably La Malinche was given to Cortés (Anderson, 2021).

Due to her noble origins, she had received a higher education than most of her people. She was a polyglot, and for that, she was very valuable to the explorer. She spoke Mayan dialects and Nahuatl, the language of the Aztecs, the great empire ruled by Moctezuma.

Cortés settled in Tabasco and took some time to get to know the region and the local people. Then, he learned that most of the tribes were subject to the Aztec Empire's domination. Cortés would take advantage of the internal political crisis of the empire to weaken them. Using La Malinche as an interpreter, he encouraged the subjugated people to rebel against the tyrant Moctezuma. The Spanish set an alliance with the Tlaxcala nation and many others and formed an army of 200,000 soldiers. Then, Cortes approached the capital city of the empire, Tenochtitlan.

La Malinche was a very intelligent woman with innate skills for strategy and war. When Cortés was negotiating with the native nations to form the alliance, La Malinche realized that the Tlaxcala were preparing a conspiracy. Those people later joined Cortés, but at first, they were fighting their own war against the Aztecs. Therefore, the leaders wanted to kill Cortés to get him out of their way. La Malinche unraveled the plan and warned Cortés, who avoided the attack (Mohammed, 2019).

Later, once in Tenochtitlan, La Malinche again had the accurate presumption of a possible attack when Cortés wasn't expecting it. As the Spanish approached Tenochtitlan, the Aztecs were warned and alert of their presence. They were aware of the league formed by the local tribes. La Malinche was in charge of intelligence before the invasion. She became a friend of an Aztec woman who gave her relevant information about an ambush they had prepared.

Warned about the plan, Cortés changed his planned route, and instead of heading directly to Tenochtitlan, he led his people to Cholula. The Aztecs believed he had supernatural powers that alerted him of the dangers or even protected him. That must have persuaded them of the divine nature of the visitors and made Moctezuma open the gates of the empire to welcome them. Cortés entered the city with only 1,000 men and found no resistance from the locals. On the contrary, they treated him like a deity. Once inside the city and having gained the emperor's trust, Cortés attacked them and defeated them within a few weeks (Mohammed, 2019).

Without La Malinche, Cortés wouldn't have arranged the alliances, would have perished under the Tlaxcala's attack, and would have walked to certain failure in Tenochtitlan. She played a decisive role in the Spanish conquests in the Yucatan peninsula. Hernán Cortés's triumph was the beginning of the expansion of the Spanish colonies in Central America.

For some people, La Malinche is the mother of the modern Mexican nation because she gave birth to Cortés's son. She contributed to building the heritage that resulted from the merging of the Native American and the Spanish components. For others, she was in part responsible for the genocide perpetrated by the Spanish conquerors within the Aztec Empire and throughout all the years the colonial occupation lasted.

Whether La Malinche betrayed her people to save herself or if she really fell in love with the Spanish conqueror is still a matter of conjecture. She indeed renounced her name and beliefs to accept the Christian name. Afterward, she had a son with Cortés, although she eventually married one of his soldiers. Later, she went with her husband to Spain, where she was welcomed with honors. After all, she could be credited for the successful defeat of Moctezuma and his empire.

Meriwether Lewis and William Clark (1800s)

After the Declaration of Independence was signed, the new government of the United States started to work on the organization of the new country. One of the objectives was to consolidate the frontiers that had been a matter of controversy. Either because they were under the control of the Native Americans or, the European powers kept sending expeditions to occupy the lands, the United States of America needed to get control of their frontiers. Some of the most desired land was that beyond the Rocky Mountains. In times of the colonies, the British, the Spanish, and the French had claimed to possess the Great Plains and the territories on the West despite the fierce resistance of the Natives. In 1803, the matter was unexpectedly solved by the purchase of the territories of Louisiana by the government of the United States from France.

President Thomas Jefferson led the diplomatic negotiation with the representatives sent by Napoleon Bonaparte, who was eager to raise funds to support his military campaigns in Europe. The purchase of Louisiana and the west of the Mississippi River increased the territory of the United States by 828,000 square miles.

Jefferson, a visionary, had anticipated some expeditions to the area and had asked the U.S. Congress for a significant sum to send a secret expedition to explore the Missouri River, establish diplomatic and commercial relationships with the local population, and find a northern corridor to the Pacific Ocean. When the purchase of Louisiana was accomplished, the expedition was ready. All Jefferson needed to do was choose the leader for the campaign, the man who would start a journey to the Pacific Ocean. His name was Meriwether Lewis, and immediately after accepting the mission, he requested the company of William Clark. Together, they would undertake a two-year journey into uncharted lands toward the Pacific.

Meriwether Lewis was born on August 18, 1774, near Charlottesville when it still belonged to the colony of Virginia. His father served in the Continental Army, and Meriwether himself enlisted as a soldier in 1794 and started a military career. By 1800, he had already achieved the rank of captain, and President Jefferson made him his personal assistant on the field. During the Northwest Campaigns in Kentucky, Indiana, and Ohio in the 1790s, Lewis served under a young officer: William Clark.

William was the son of a tobacco plantation owner from Virginia. After independence, the family moved to Kentucky. There, William was engaged in the American–Indian conflicts in the frontier of the Ohio territories. Then, William entered the army and played a key role in leading the Chosen Rifle Company. In that context, the two heroes from Virginia met and became endearing friends. When Meriwether called William to include him in the expedition to the West, Clark was at home taking care of his health, but couldn't refuse the invitation from his best friend.

Meriwether was assigned the rank of captain of the expedition, and although he claimed the same role as his partner, the Army denied it. Nonetheless, both of them secretly agreed to refer to each other as captains. They organized the crew for the expedition and named it the

Corps of Discovery. The crew consisted of about 40 men, and they carried keelboats and pirogues to sail up the stream of the Missouri. Until then, all the water routes encompassed the Mississippi basin and led to the Gulf of Mexico, to the Southeast, and ended in the Atlantic Ocean. The Corps of Discovery had to follow the Missouri and try to find a connection with the other side of the continent through a north-west route.

The expeditionary team officially started their journey on May 14, 1804, moving ahead from Camp Wood. They made slow progress as they had to pull the vessels and then paddle until the trading post of Fort Mandan. There, they settled in a camp to pass the winter.

In the spring of 1805, the melting of the snow of the Rocky Mountains brought favorable waters for the expeditionary crew. They sailed up the Missouri through one of the tributary rivers, the present-day Jefferson River. On their way, they ran into the Shoshone tribe, which guided them to pass through the mountains. There, they couldn't take their vessels with them and, instead, made that part of their trip on horses. Later, they had to assemble canoe vessels to continue their trip by water.

In September 1804, the expedition ran into the Lakota Sioux nation in South Dakota, who were settled where the Bad Rivers joined the Missouri. They most likely had to camp there to wait for the end of winter. Then, the Lakota saw the strangers in their region. The tribe had already established commercial bonds with the British, and the presence of the Americans was perceived as a threat.

The Native people were determined to stop the expedition and prevent the Americans from using their lands to trade or as a passage. Eventually, the Lakota chief, Black Buffalo, received the foreigners and understood they were more interested in moving forward and perhaps trading than taking lands or engaging in war. Thus, the Corps was allowed to continue.

They reached the Bitterroot Mountains, and from there, Lewis and Clark guided the team downstream until reaching the mouth of the Columbia River, which opened to the Pacific Ocean. The goal was accomplished. In September 1806, Lewis and Clark returned to St.

Louis and brought Jefferson the good news. They had found a water route as the president had anticipated.

Besides reaching the Pacific, Lewis and Clark accomplished all the objectives President Jefferson had set before the expedition was approved by the government. The Corps of Discovery effectively established positive diplomatic relationships with the Native tribes they met on their way. They were able to reinforce the commercial exchange of furs, which had been an important activity since colonial times. The tribes welcomed the expedition with food, shelter, and guidance through the unknown territory.

In addition to this, the explorers brought back a lot of relevant information not only about the people beyond the frontier or about the population of the country, but they also brought complete and vivid descriptions of the wildlife of the territories, the species of plants and animals, and the resources that could be found there. William Clark was a talented draftsman and used his skills to draw detailed maps of all the regions covered during the journey. He took note of creeks and rivers, with exhaustive descriptions and names, pointing out the shapes of the shores and the landscapes. He even registered the places where the Corps had established the camps. These maps and thorough information were most useful for future expeditions to the West.

After the end of the expedition, Meriwether Lewis was rewarded with 1,600 acres of public land for his contribution to the enforcement of the state and accomplishing his mission. In 1807, Jefferson assigned him as the governor of the Territory of Upper Louisiana, although during the first years, it was almost impossible to keep the region under control. In addition to his place in public office, Lewis endeavored to prepare the publishing of a book about the expedition. He died only two years later while he was on his way to Washington to explain the expenditures of his administration. The circumstances of his death were surrounded by mystery. All that is known is that he received a gunshot (Buckley, 2023a).

On his end, Clark received the same financial compensation and was appointed as the brigadier general of militia for the Louisiana (later Missouri) Territory by President Jefferson. He was in charge of the building of Fort Osage on the Missouri River and became a promoter of trading in the area. Later, he assumed public office as the governor of Missouri, and President Monroe commissioned him to lead the diplomatic relationship with the Native population. He arranged the Treaty of Portage des Sioux in 1815 and supervised the reallocation of the tribes outside the state. Nonetheless, he advocated for peaceful coexistence between the White and the Native communities.

Together, Meriwether Lewis and William Clark contributed to spreading the limits of the United States and made it a greater country, not only regarding the extension of the territory but also the resources, the economic activity, and the integration of the different people who lived in it. They also helped shape the new nation and develop a modern state.

Amelia Earhart and George Putnam (1900s)

For centuries, societies have assigned women certain roles and have established that certain activities aren't feminine. Women have been deprived of many civil and political rights for ages until they achieved equal status to men. However, there are many other gender biases that consider women too weak or fragile for some sports and jobs. However, some women never believed in what society told them they could or couldn't do. Amelia Earhart was definitely one of them. She trusted more in her instinct and was ready to follow her inner wishes rather than what others had to say. Fortunately, Amelia met someone who saw her for what she really was and joined her in amazing adventures.

Her full name was Amelia Mary Earhart, and she was born on July 24, 1897. She lived the first years of her life in Kansas but later moved to Chicago and Pennsylvania. When she was a child, girls weren't expected to do important things like flying a plane. In fact, planes were just being invented.

The first plane was invented by the Wright brothers, who accomplished their first flight in 1903. A few years later, Amelia saw a plane for the first time. At the time, it didn't make a great impression.

She said it was just wood and wires. Some years later, she changed her mind. While she was still at college, she went to Canada to visit her sister. By then, World War I had broken out, and Amelia wanted to help. So, she left college and joined the military hospital to volunteer as a nurse. During her time at the hospital, she met many aviators who inspired her interest in planes.

After the war, Amelia went back to college to study medicine in New York. However, she had to move to California with her parents. That very year, she had an experience that would change her life. Her father took her to an air show in Long Beach, and there, she was invited by a pilot to take a real flight. The moment the plane left the ground, Amelia knew she had to fly.

Against all the odds, Amelia enrolled to take flying lessons and also started saving money. Within a year, she bought her first plane. It was a Kinner Airster biplane she called "The Canary" because it was painted yellow. By 1924, she had already completed her flying lessons. Just by doing that, Amelia had gone further than what was expected of women, but that was just the preparation for great feats.

In October 1922, Amelia set her first worldwide record. She took part in an air meeting at Los Angeles' Rogers Airfield and became the first woman to fly at 14,000 feet, the highest altitude reached at the time. But not everything would be so easy. Between 1924 and 1928, Amelia had to attend to her family's financial struggles. She sold her plane and took many different jobs (Monteil, 2022).

However, people like Amelia are called to do great things. In 1928, her life took a turn again when she met a publisher who was at the zenith of his career. His name was George Putnam, and he worked for a prestigious company. His last book was a blockbuster, and his name had become popular. He had launched *We*, a book which told Charles Lindbergh's adventures in his solo flight from New York to Paris, and it was quickly becoming one of the most important nonfiction bestsellers.

Perhaps for the matter of his last success, George was in contact with important people from the aviation world. In 1928, a wealthy man from the United States contacted him to sponsor the first flight over the Atlantic Ocean with a woman pilot. George accepted the offer and was dedicated to finding the perfect candidate. Soon, he heard the name of Amelia Earhart, who was already well-known for her personal record a few years earlier.

George found Amelia and extended her the proposal to be the first woman ever to fly over the ocean. Amelia accepted the offer with enthusiasm, although it didn't go exactly as she expected. She completed the flight but as a passenger. The plane piloted by Wilmer Stultz and Louis Gordon departed Trepassey, Newfoundland, Canada, on June 17, 1928. The plane landed in Wales after 20 hours in the air. Amelia got off the airplane and, despite not being the pilot, became a symbol of what women could do.

After the flight, George Putnam offered Amelia the opportunity to write a book about her flight. He was excited about the outcomes of his previous work, and he was also captivated by Amelia. However, they didn't start a relationship until he got divorced from his first wife. George and Amelia got married in 1931.

Amelia had some liberal ideas about marriage, which were quite different from most girls of her time. She wanted to dedicate her life to planes and finding new records to beat. George agreed completely with that and supported her career. He asked her to marry him and give him just one year; if she wasn't happy, they would get divorced. Amelia accepted his proposal but kept her maiden name. After the flight over the Atlantic Ocean, she became a celebrity.

Back in the United States, she was invited to visit the White House, and she had the chance to meet the president. Cosmopolitan Magazine offered her a job as an editor on aviation issues, and she even starred in advertisements for popular products.

Putnam published the book about her flight entitled *20 Hrs., 40 Min*, which was a success as he had predicted. He led a campaign to promote the book and took Amelia on a tour, giving lectures and conferences about her adventures, dreams, and projects. She was an inspiration for other women. It wasn't common in the 1920s to see a woman being the successful one that kept all the attention, and the husband being at her side. Nonetheless, George Putnam was proud of his wife and accepted with joy to be called "Mr. Earhart."

Amelia didn't allow fame to blind her and immediately set new goals for herself. She wanted the honor of being the first woman to cross the ocean. So, she arranged a flight over the Atlantic, but this time, she was the pilot. Her plane departed Harbour Grace, Newfoundland, and landed in Londonderry, Northern Ireland, in May 1932. It lasted 14 hours and 56 minutes, a new record for the world and for herself. The original plan was to land in Paris, but a series of mechanical problems and bad weather conditions forced her to change course. George Putnam organized a tour across the country so Amelia could tell everybody about her experience. In 1932, the couple published *The Fun of It*, a book with memories of Amelia's flights.

Three years later, Amelia set another record. She became the first woman to fly alone over the Pacific Ocean. She flew from Honolulu, Hawaii, to California, on January 11, 1935. The 17 hours and 7 minutes flight covered 2,408 miles, a longer distance than the flights over the Atlantic. Amelia seemed to be unstoppable. After this accomplishment, she still had one more goal, a very ambitious one: She wanted to complete the first flight around the world. Her husband supported her idea as he always had.

Amelia asked Fred Noonan to be her navigator, and together prepared the plane. It was a twin-engine Lockheed Electra. The roadmap for a 29,000-mile journey wasn't easy. They had to calculate the time and distance to source fuel and the essential goods for the trip. They couldn't take much in the little plane. Amelia and Fred left Miami on June 1, 1937, and headed East. Their last stop was in New Guinea. The plane departed toward Howland Island on July 2nd. They were flying across the Pacific Ocean the last time Amelia communicated with the U.S. Coast Guard on the radio. She said, "We are running north and south," and then communication was lost. They never found the plane, and it is still unknown what happened to Amelia.

George Putnam published Amelia's biography in 1939. *Soaring Wings: A Biography of Amelia Earhart* was a compilation of letters and personal memories Amelia had once written. Her name continues to be a feminist icon that represents all the challenging and threatening things women are capable of doing. Amelia has been an inspiration for generations of women who have dared to be aviators and many other professions that were mistakenly considered only for men.

Edmund Hillary and Tenzing Norgay (1900s)

Every person has dreamed of being at the top of the world at least once in their lives. Edmund and Tenzing can credit themselves for having achieved it for real, and, besides, for being the first people to do it. They defied the most extreme natural conditions to climb to the ceiling of the world. This is the story of two men who worked together to master the highest mountain on Earth in times when there wasn't sophisticated equipment either to protect themselves or to guide them on their path. Teamwork and mutual trust were the pillars of a risky and unforgettable feat.

To hit the summit of Mount Everest was a serious matter. It wasn't about a sports accomplishment for hikers. It was about national pride. Different countries had attempted to take their teams higher than the rest since 1921 when the British led the first failed attempt. There were also individual adventures, but that was a huge mistake. Reaching the highest peak of the Himalayan could only be achieved in a team of two. The British were determined to claim that honor, beating even the experienced Swiss alpinists, and the French, who already had permission for an expedition. The glory of being the first to reach the summit had to be for Great Britain.

In the spring of 1953, a British expedition led by Sir John Hunt landed at the base of Everest. The crew included 350 porters and 20 Sherpas, nomadic people from Nepal who could guide the climbers up the slopes of the mountains. The team had many climbers, but only 10 would be elected as potential summiteers, and those 10 would go in pairs. Edmund Hillary was one of those summiteers, and Tenzing Norgay was his partner.

Tenzing Norgay was an experienced Sherpa. The word "Sherpa" is the name of a cast that means "man from the East" (Rand, 1954). People from the West who went to the town at the steep slope of Everest and asked them for guidance and shelter, know them for the service they could provide. The Chomo-Lungma (as the Tibetans call Mount Everest) is the natural environment of the Sherpas (*Hillary and Norgay reach Everest summit*, n.d.).

The world knew him as Tenzing Norgay, but it is unclear if that was actually his name. The Sherpas don't use surnames as Western people do. Both words are in his native language of Darjeeling, the little town between India and Nepal where he lived. The word "tenzing" means "thought holder," and "norgay" means "increasing wealth" (Rand, 1954). It is also unknown when he was born. Sherpas didn't have birth registers in Darjeeling. He could have been born in 1914, perhaps, on May 15th in the Khumbu region in Nepal (Encyclopaedia Britannica, 2023n). What is known about his life is what he told everybody who went to meet him after his feat, overcoming the difficulties of English, a very different language from his own.

He reached Darjeeling when he was a teenager after running away from his parents' home. He established in the town and became, like most of the inhabitants, a Sherpa. He was only 19 when he joined and guided the first expedition, and in 1935, it was the first time he took part in an expedition to Everest. He became an expert and became the man with the most excursions to the highest mountain on earth.

In 1952, he achieved a great accomplishment that made his name stand out among the other Sherpas. He joined the Swiss expedition that reached the highest altitude up to that point so far. Tenzing Norgay and his partner, alpinist Raymond Lambert, climbed 28,210 feet before turning back because they ran out of supplies. If there was a Sherpa who already knew the route to reach the summit of the Chomo-Lungma, that was Tenzing Norgay.

Edmund Percival Hillary was born on July 20, 1919, in Auckland, New Zealand. His first experiences climbing were in New Zealand, in the Southern Alps, while he was still a schoolboy. He served in the military forces of his country during World War II on the Allies' side. After the war, he was back in his country and was climbing again. That was the moment when he decided to climb Everest.

In 1953, Edmund was invited to join the British team. He was 33 years old and was in excellent shape. He was trained and skilled. That one was the fourth expedition to the Himalayas in the past two years; the perfect prospect to be elected as a summiteer.

The beginning of the expedition was tough. Despite the time of the year, the weather conditions were extremely hostile, and the team members struggled to acclimatize. Commander Hunt wanted to reach the South Col, the place where the last successful Swiss expedition had been. Eventually, after 12 long days, the team reached the location and set up camp. Then, Hunt had to decide who would be the first pair to venture to the summit.

Even though Hillary was ready and Tenzing Norgay was by far the most experienced, Hunt decided to send Tom Bourdillon and Charles Evans first. They climbed the South Summit, but when they were just 330 feet away from their main objective, the highest peak, they were forced to come back. As they explained later, it was a difficult decision because they were close to accomplishing the goal. However, Evans was exhausted, and they both knew they were struggling to breathe (*Sir Edmund Hillary*, 2013).

With the first team back at the camp, Hunt had to decide who he would send next. Then, Hillary and Tenzing became the chosen team. Their own adventure started three days later after the first two climbers had returned.

The climb to the top wasn't exempt from obstacles and dangers. At one point, after surpassing South Summit, where Evans and Bourdillon had reached, Hillary and Norgay found an abrupt rocky spur that opened in front of them just before the real summit. They had to use their axes to climb through it and finally reach the top of the world. It was 11:30 in the morning of May 29th. For the first time in history, men reached the summit of Mount Everest and came back to tell it.

Hillary stretched out his hand to congratulate his partner, but Tenzing Norgay, unaware of British courtesy and excited for their accomplishment, hugged him in response. It is argued that after the first seconds of emotion and joy, controversies arise to determine which of them actually arrived first at the summit. But those speculations came from the press and the people who read the news. They, the real two who shared that odyssey, always said they reached the summit together (Rand, 1954). Perhaps there was indeed a winner, but the only way to achieve that accomplishment was with the support of a partner. Edmund and Tenzing could be credited for that.

Hillary and Norgay only stood on the top of Everest for 15 minutes. Hillary said later that at the summit, he searched for any evidence of other summiteers having been there before, including his partners, who had never come back. Unfortunately, there was no trace of them. They descended and gathered with the team. Hillary's first words to the partner who came to encounter them were: "Well, George, we knocked the bastard off!" (*Sir Edmund Hillary*, 2013).

The two mountaineers became celebrities all around the world. They were awarded by the British Crown. Edmund Hillary was knighted, and Norgay, who wasn't a citizen of a country member of the Commonwealth, received the British Empire Medal.

Besides the personal glory of the two summiteers, the feat had a great impact on the local community. From the moment Hillary and Norgay summited Everest, hundreds of expeditions have been carried out. It was a formidable impulse for the region as a tourist attraction. It has also represented the opportunity for the Sherpas to improve their living conditions. Until then, they were hired under the visitors' terms. The role Norgay played as a teammate to Hillary proved their knowledge and expertise was irreplaceable.

Chapter 4:

Pop Culture Duos

Mark Antony and Cleopatra (50 B.C.E)

Even though they were historical figures who disputed power in the most powerful empires of Antiquity, their intense and unfortunate relationship has transcended history books. Mark Antony and Cleopatra lived a love story that could only be found in a novel or a Greek tragedy, and still, they were the two more prominent leaders of their respective people. Antony dared to challenge the power of Caesar, and Cleopatra proved that women have always been made to rule. The mighty Queen of the Nile had all to rule the ancient world, and Mark Antony had the guts to confront the new emperor, but the alliance between them would only lead to death. Their story has been taken to arts and literature over and over again throughout time. Here is the real story.

During the 1st century B.C.E., Rome had spread its domains to most parts of the known world in Europe, Eastern Asia, and North Africa under the rule of Julius Caesar. During his campaigns to consolidate his power, he met and had a love affair with the powerful queen of Egypt. That was Cleopatra.

She was only 20 years old when she met Julius Caesar, but by then, she was already a pharaoh (king or queen for the Egyptians). Pop culture depicts Cleopatra as an Egyptian, but the truth is that she came from a foreign land. Cleopatra IV was the daughter of King Ptolemy XII Auletes, a member of the Macedonian dynasty that ruled Egypt since the time Alexander the Great conquered the nation in 323 B.C.E. (Tyldesley, 2023). Later, the Egyptian kingdom would be annexed in 30 B.C.E. to the Roman Empire like the rest of what once was the

Macedonian Empire. The destiny of Cleopatra and her kingdom were inextricably woven.

Around the year 50 B.C.E., Cleopatra had to fight against her brother, who had occupied the throne. She fled to Syria, and there, she organized an army to seize power, and she searched for an alliance with Rome. That is how she met Julius Caesar and established much more than a political alliance with him. They became lovers, and Cleopatra had a son with him, Ptolemy Caesar. Caesar took her to Rome after he stopped the civil war that questioned his power. The Egyptian queen was living in his own village and was in Rome when he was murdered in a conspiracy.

Despite Cleopatra's claim of Ptolemy Caesar being the true natural heir to Julius Caesar, without Caesar, her position in Rome was delicate. So, she left and took her son back to her kingdom. However, during her stay in Rome, she had the opportunity to meet one of Julius Caesar's men of trust. His name was Mark Anthony.

Marcus Antonius was his name in Latin. He was born in Egypt and belonged to a family of politicians. He was a soldier in Julius Caesar's army and also a member of the triumvirate. During the years of civil war, Mark Anthony had a seat in the Senate and was one the fiercest defenders of Julius Caesar. After Julius Caesar's death, Mark Anthony gained power in the government, but he was soon challenged by Octavian, Caesar's adoptive son and appointed heir. Therefore, Mark Anthony turned against him and tried to seize power.

Mark Anthony and Cleopatra had a common interest: They both believed they had the right to take power in Rome. That was the main reason why they searched for an alliance. However, once again, Cleopatra would provoke much more than a political coalition.

The meeting was arranged in Tarsus, a city on the coasts of present-day Turkey, where Mark Anthony had established his army. Cleopatra attended the encounter with all pageantry, dressed like Goddess Aphrodite, trying to make a deep impression on the Roman leader. She needed his support to regain power. Mark Anthony was indeed captivated by the queen. Whether they genuinely fell in love, or their relationship was framed by the mutual need for military support has been left to historians and popular imagination. They started a love affair and joined forces to attack Rome, confront Octavian, and seize the throne.

The couple settled in Alexandria, in the Egyptian Empire. Mark Anthony left his wife in Italy to stay with the queen. There, he didn't treat her as a protected vassal kingdom but as an independent monarch. Mark Anthony and Cleopatra had twins, Alexander Helios and Cleopatra Selene.

Despite the happy family life, neither of them had forgotten their deep power aspirations. Thus, Mark Anthony returned to Italy and attempted to negotiate his position with Octavian, who had become the Emperor. Mark Anthony agreed to marry Octavian's sister as his first wife had died, and there was no formal bond between him and Cleopatra. However, as time passed by, Mark Anthony understood that his marriage of convenience was taking him nowhere. Therefore, he decided to go back to Alexandria.

Cleopatra took him back as she still needed his support to recover the lands that had been part of the Macedonian kingdom. Mark Anthony still needed Egyptian support if he wanted to have some of his old power back in Italy. Together, they formed an army in Alexandria and launched a successful expedition in present-day Armenia, where they defeated Octavian's forces. Afterward, Cleopatra was acclaimed as Queen of Kings, and her son, Ptolemy Caesar (recognized then as Mark Anthony's son), was given the title of King of Kings. They were challenging Roman supremacy.

Despite Cleopatra's wealth and Mark Anthony's military genius, their alliance couldn't compete with Octavian's professional army. They quickly surrounded Alexandria, and there was little hope for the couple. It is believed that Cleopatra tried to negotiate with Octavian without Mark Anthony being aware of it. It was her last attempt to obtain forgiveness for her children. While Mark Anthony was on the battlefield, his men, one by one, deserted him.

If they were cornered, they planned to commit suicide. Cleopatra wanted to try Mark Anthony's loyalty and faked her death. When he received the news of Cleopatra's death, he let himself fall over his sword, which passed through his body. He was still alive when he was taken to Cleopatra. Even though she had thought he would follow her if she was dead, she was deeply impressed to see her lover couldn't bear losing her.

After Mark Anthony died, Cleopatra committed suicide herself. She made her servants bring her an asp, a symbol of royalty and divinity. She made the snake bite her and died soon due to the powerful poison.

Most of the memories of Cleopatra and Mark Anthony are linked to their tragic love story framed by ambition and pursuit of power. Nonetheless, it is worth remembering that Cleopatra was a queen in times when women were limited to domestic issues. She was able to create strong political alliances and subjugated the greatest power of her time. Cleopatra was also a woman who excelled in many ways. As the daughter of a king, she had a thorough education. She was a polyglot and was also keen on chemistry. She knew about poisons and plant extracts and made important contributions to the development of medicine (Le Beau Lucchesi, 2022). Under her rule, the Egyptian Empire lived an era of splendor and progress.

Romeo and Juliet (1600s)

This fictional duo has become the best metaphor for love. Any mention of the names immediately brings the other to one's mind. These characters created by the superb pen of one of the most influential playwrights of all time, William Shakespeare, have transcended literature. Everybody knows something about Romeo and Juliet, and it continues to be the preferred reference in movies, songs, and even daily talk. But what not everybody knows is that their story isn't completely fictional. It is based on real people who lived in Verona. Of course, the details were added by the writer's imagination. It isn't necessary to have read the play to know it is the most romantic and tragic love story ever. Nonetheless, their unfortunate destiny was also a reflection of the society of the writer's time and a message about intolerance and pride.

Romeo and Juliet is a play written by Shakespeare between 1594 and 1596, but it first appeared in 1597 to be performed for Queen Elizabeth I. She was an enthusiast of theater, which flourished under her reign.

Shakespeare's play was a depiction of Elizabethan society. However, the play was Shakespeare's version of a poem written by another English writer, which was a translation from the French of an old Italian tale. This tale, it is believed, was the story of the real characters that passed through generations by oral tradition until someone wrote it down. That man was Luigi Da Porto, a man from Vicenza (Venice) who heard it from a villager from Verona (Teso, 2015). However, it is Shakespeare, thanks to his talent and his fame in Great Britain, who was credited for bringing Romeo and Juliet to life.

The story between Romeo and Juliet—the real and the fictional— happened in Verona, an Italian city, at the beginning of the 14th century. Italy wasn't a unified country then but a group of principalities. There was a tough division among the citizens between those who supported the Pope and those who stood on the emperor's side. Shakespeare represented that division with the rivalry between two of the most prominent families of the city: the Montagues and the Capulets. There is a palace in the center of Verona that has been identified as the house of the Capulets, and every year, thousands of tourists visit the place where it all began, the love story and the myth.

According to Shakespeare's version, Juliet was a 14-year-old teenager who belonged to the Capulet family. Her parents had arranged her marriage with a noble named Paris without the girl's consent. In Shakespeare's time, life expectancy was very low, so it was very common for women to get married and become mothers at an early age. It was also common for parents to arrange convenient marriages to ensure a position for the daughters in a medieval society where women couldn't work and would be condemned to poverty and exclusion if they didn't have a large inheritance. Juliet didn't want to marry a man she didn't love, but that was her destiny.

In the Elizabethan era, plays were inspired by Greek tragedies. The characters had to face an unavoidable terrible destiny they couldn't choose and couldn't change. If they tried to defy destiny, tragedy unfolded on them. For Juliet, her parents sealed her destiny. This type of play was used to educate the audience and spread a strong moral message of obedience.

Juliet's family was at war with the Montagues. There was no way she could have known that at a masque ball at her own house, she would meet and fall in love with the son of her family's deadly enemy. His name was Romeo, and before his encounter with Juliet, he was madly in love with a girl named Rosalia who didn't love him.

The night of the ball, Romeo ventured to enter the house of his enemies with his cousins, Benvolio and Mercutio, because he was told Rosalia was invited to the masquerade. They were wearing masks, so they believed they could be at the party without being discovered. Instead of finding Rosalia, Romeo sees Juliet and falls in love with her instantly. Juliet also received Cupid's arrow.

Shakespeare then painted the picture of the perfect love when he wrote the scene at Juliet's balcony. There, she believes she is alone and expresses her love for Romeo. She didn't know it, but the young man was hiding in the garden. He appeared to confess he loved her too and proposed to marry her even though they had met just 24 hours ago. They knew their families wouldn't approve of their love, so they decided to keep it secret.

According to the story, Romeo found a Friar ready to risk his reputation and his own life to help the hero and heroine who wanted to ignore the voice of reason to let passion guide them. Friar Lawrence joined them in sacred matrimony. Then, tragedy unleashed.

Juliet's father, unaware of his daughter's secret marriage to a Montague, arranged her wedding with Paris as it was established. Juliet fell into despair and ran to Friar Lawrence to ask for help. The man came up with a terrible plan. He gave the young girl a beverage to fake her death. She would be deeply asleep for 24 hours, and she would then wake up. Her family would take her to the pantheon and leave her inert body, and then she would be free to be with her true love. Nothing could go wrong.

Friar Lawrence sent a herald to warn Romeo about the plan, but the message never reached its destiny. Juliet followed the friar's instructions to the very detail, and as he had predicted, her body was left at the graveyard.

Romeo heard the news of Juliet's death, and he had no way to know it was a performance. He bought some poison from a street vendor and went to the Capulet's pantheon. There, he found the rigid and cold body of his beloved. He believed she was truly dead and drank the poison that killed him in the instant. Just then, Juliet woke up and found Romeo lying dead beside her. She couldn't bear it and took his own dagger and killed herself. Like in Greek tragedies, those who attempt to challenge their fate can only find death. At the same time, both families received a cruel punishment for all the pain they had caused with their rivalry.

This is the story, as Luigi Da Porto once wrote, and that has reached the present through Shakespeare's eyes and imagination. It is impossible to know which of those elements were fictional and what part of the story was true. However, these two teenagers became the hero and heroine in a society framed by cold interests and status differences that were more important than feelings.

This duo might not have changed the world like other duos in this book, but they have transcended time. If their names and their story that dates from so long ago have survived, it is because they reflect a side of human nature. Perhaps the pursuit of a perfect love capable of everything and ready to perform any sacrifice. Even if the writer didn't attempt to, Romeo and Juliet's romance became the stereotype of romantic love in Western society.

Frida Kahlo and Diego Rivera (1900s)

If Romeo and Juliet's romance is the image of perfect love, the romantic story between Frida and Diego represents love in all nonconventional ways. Each of them had made a name for themselves as important and influential painters who represented a point of inflection in the arts. Moreover, both of them were disruptive characters who challenged the morality of their society and embraced revolutionary ideas to promote social change. However, despite their artistic and political influence, they have also transcended as a couple who reinvented love to make it fit who they were and how they wanted to live their lives. It was a tumultuous love, with many vicissitudes, but in the end, they helped each other to find the most genuine version of themselves. Together, they wrote a significant page of the history of their country and of humankind.

Frida's life was marked by tragedy when she was very young. She was born on July 6, 1907, in Coyoacán, Mexico. Her mother was a Spanish and Native Mexican descendant, and her father was German. It is important to note her origins because she became an icon for Latin American women who found in Frida and her paintings a depiction of their native image, and the pride for being so.

When Frida was a little child, she became ill with polio, and that left her with permanent disabilities. She was slightly limp and suffered a chronic ailment all of her life. Years later, she was traveling in a bus when it crashed with another vehicle. Frida was one of the most severely injured passengers. An iron rod passed through her body and drilled her pelvis. She also had several fractures in her spine and ribs. She miraculously lived, but the terrible accident left her prostrated for months. She had more than 30 surgeries in her life. While she was in bed, practically immobilized during her slow recovery, she started to paint. She was an autodidact.

Through her paintings, she expressed the pain in her body and her soul. Most of her paintings were self-portraits. Her style was characterized as a naïve-folk art, and the main themes she covered in her works were linked to Mexican society. Frida depicted the different ethnic elements that coexisted but also denounced colonial and gender oppression. If her paintings were in great part an autobiography through images instead of words, they were also the way Frida expressed her political revolutionary ideas.

Before the accident, she had entered the National Preparatory School in Mexico City. There, a man was painting a mural. His name was Diego Rivera. At that moment, she didn't know their lives would be linked forever, but sometimes, she would sit and watch him work on the mural called *The Creation*. She told her friends she would marry that man someday (*Frida Kahlo biography*, n.d.).

Diego didn't notice her at first. He was much older than Frida; he was born on December 8, 1886, in Guanajuato, Mexico. By 1922, when he came to paint at Frida's school, he was a renowned artist. He had studied art in an academy in Mexico City at the age of 10, and he was so talented that the governor of Veracruz assigned him a scholarship to continue his studies in Europe. He was in Spain and France and was in touch with the most relevant painters of the moment. He became friends with Pablo Picasso and George Braque.

Following the influence of these vanguardist painters, Diego first adopted Cubism for his art, but later, he developed a style of his own, framed by another artistic movement: post-impressionism. However, Diego and his friend Alfaro Siqueiros are considered the precursors of muralism and created a unique style regarding aesthetics and meaning.

In 1921, Diego was back in Mexico and was soon influenced by the ideas of the Mexican Revolution. He was inspired by the popular leaders Pancho Villa and Emiliano Zapata, who fought against the elitism of the local oligarchy and represented the oppressed classes of Mexico, mainly peasants and indigenous people. They became the subjects of Diego's painting, and he used his art as a means to support the revolution. His paintings about different moments of his country's history became representative pieces of national art.

The fresco *The Creation* at the National Preparatory School was his first important mural. He endeavored in that work when Frida saw him for the first time, but it wasn't until 1928 that he met her. She had joined the Communist Party, where Diego was already a member. They met at a meeting, and Frida asked him to review some of her paintings. They fell in love and started a relationship against Frida's parents' will. She was 20 years younger than him. After a short and intense romance, the couple got married. Frida's father called them "the elephant and the dove."

As a married couple, they both continued with their careers, but Frida had to move following Diego's job. He was appointed to paint his murals in important places. First, in San Diego, California, and later, he was called to paint the entrance of the Rockefeller Center in New York. The mural was named Man at the Crossroads, and Rivera introduced the image of Vladimir Lenin, the Russian Communist leader. The Rockefeller Center's manager didn't agree with Diego's choice for the painting, which hadn't been meaningless at all, and halted the work. Due to this incident, Frida and Diego went back to Mexico.

Despite their profound mutual love, their relationship was very unusual. They lived many years in separate homes, and Diego had many love affairs, including with Frida's sister. Even though she knew about her husband's infidelities, and she seemed eager to forgive him every time, the entanglement with her own sister caused her deep pain. However, there was always a new beginning for the couple.

Frida also had many romantic relationships with other people while being married. One of the most resounding was a brief affair with the Communist leader Leon Trotsky. Frida and Diego hosted Trotsky and his wife in their own house while they were in Mexico, running away from political persecution.

Diego and Frida became renowned painters among the most prestigious vanguard artists of their time. Frida traveled to Europe and met some of the greatest names in painting. André Breton, a leading representative of Surrealism, told Frida her style was surrealistic. She held exhibitions in the most important galleries of Mexico and New York, and the Louvre included one of her paintings.

Their love story continued throughout all of their lives, filled with ups and downs, excesses, and forgiveness. In 1939, Frida was invited to Paris, where she spent several months. Then, she decided to divorce Diego. However, after she came back to Mexico, they got married again in 1940. Their love had no remedy.

Frida's health was very weak, and by 1950, she was diagnosed with gangrene in one of her feet. From then on, she spent most of her time at the hospital and was almost immobilized. Nonetheless, she continued to paint and had a solo exhibition in 1953. She passed away on July 13, 1954, in her Blue House. Diego lived a few more years. He died on November 25, 1957.

Diego Rivera and Frida Kahlo are two prominent names in American art. Each of them left an enduring footprint due to their style and their political commitment. However, Frida has surpassed him, and her influence has become greater throughout the years. She has become a symbol of the Native American woman, and her art represents women's struggle even beyond her own country.

Nonetheless, Frida herself has become a pop culture character. Her face and some of her most popular paintings can be found anywhere: Her paintings decorate walls of buildings in distant corners of the world, and her face is printed on clothes. She has become a fashion symbol, even for those who aren't familiar with her work or her story. Even so, her legacy will continue to endure, just as her love story with Diego.

Chapter 5:

Revolutionary Duos

Vladimir Lenin and Trotsky (1800s–1900s)

By the end of the 19th century, the world was going through a period of modernization enabled by the Second Industrial Revolution. Most countries in Europe had passed through deep social changes that had widened civil rights for people as a means to control the social unrest caused by the capitalist system.

Meanwhile, the Russian Empire seemed to be frozen in time. The economy hadn't developed as the others on the continent, and most parts of the population lived in an unequal and unfair feudal society under terrible conditions. The tsar represented the archaic structures of absolutism and autocratic power. Because of this, the revolutionary ideas that Marx and Engels had spread in 1848 resonated among the Russian workers. Two political leaders, Vladimir Lenin and Leon Trotsky, had assumed control of the Russian Communist Party and would try time after time to conduct a revolution that would end the current system. They just had to wait for their opportunity.

Leon Trotsky wasn't his real name but his pseudonym. His real name was Lev Davidovich Bronshtein, and he was born on November 7, 1879, in Yanovka, which is present-day Ukraine. At that time, it was a part of the Russian Empire. Even though Leon was born to a wealthy Jewish family of farmers, he was moved by the bad living conditions of peasants and workers.

His political activism started when he was still very young. When he went to study at Nikolayev, he learned about the ideas of Marxism. He entered the University of Odessa but didn't stay there long. Instead, he came back to Nikolayev. He joined a group of workers who were secretly organizing the South Russian Workers' Union. He was arrested in 1898 for insurrectional activities and deported as a prisoner to Siberia. This was an extensive and hostile territory in the northeast where political prisoners were forced to pay for their crimes.

While he was in Siberia, he married Aleksandra Sokolovskaya, a partner in the movement who was caught with him. Lev escaped from prison in 1902 and got a passport that helped him leave the country. It belonged to Leon Trotsky, and that was the name he adopted from then on. Leon was ready to engage in a new operation to boost revolution. He embarked on a trip to London to gather with the representatives of the Russian Social Democrats, who ran a newspaper called *Iskra* (*The Spark*) used to spread the ideals of the revolution. The head of the group was Vladimir Ulyanov, better known as Lenin.

Vladimir Ilich Ulyanov was born on April 10, 1870, in Simbirsk, Russia. Like Trotsky, he changed his name to protect his identity as he was a fugitive. He was exiled to Siberia in 1901 due to his underground party activities. His family wasn't economically comfortable, but Vladimir's parents were highly educated. His father was a schoolteacher, and later an inspector, and his mother was the daughter of a physician. Vladimir was a skilled student and graduated from school with high honors.

Two tragic incidents marked his life and turned him into an active revolutionary. His father was forced into an early retirement due to a spreading fear of education that could challenge a reactionary system as it was. Later, Vladimir's eldest brother was hanged, accused of conspiracy, and was never given a fair trial. The name was permanently associated with a "state criminal" (Resis, 2023). Later, Vladimir entered Imperial Kazan University to study law but was banned a few months later, accused of insurrectional activities with other students.

After some time in Samara and outside the country, making contact with Marxist thinkers of Europe, Vladimir joined a group of Marxists to organize the Union for the Struggle for the Liberation of the Working Class in Moscow. In 1895, all the members of the group were imprisoned, and Lenin was sent to Siberia until 1901. After leaving prison, he fled abroad and settled in London, where he, along with other Marxist activists, worked on the newspaper.

In 1905, the Marxist group led a revolution against the Tsarist autocracy. Leon Trotsky was one of the delegates who commanded the operation. The revolution was suffocated by the imperial forces, and Trotsky was again deported to Siberia, and again was able to escape, this time to Vienna, where he lived until 1914 when World War I broke out. Then he was again deported, this time to the United States, where he remained until 1917.

Meanwhile, Lenin wasn't in Russia when the revolution arose in 1905. Instead, he was in Switzerland, and, therefore, didn't take direct action. However, he devoted himself to outlining the strategy for a future successful revolution. From the beginning, there were deep ideological differences between Lenin and Trotsky and all the other members of the Communist Party, which would have consequences in the future.

In 1914, World War I unfolded. The tsar declared war on Germany and the Austro-Hungarian Empire, and for over three years, Russian soldiers were forced to fight on the battlefront. The winter of 1916–1917 was particularly tough for the Russians. Even though they had a large army, they confronted well-equipped and better-trained German soldiers on the East front. Weakened, wounded, and mutilated soldiers populated the cities, and the rest of the population was starving. It was an untenable situation.

The Communist Party had expressed opposition to the war from the beginning. They claimed it was a war where workers were sent to the front to kill each other. Instead, they should join their forces against the capitalist system that oppressed them. However, the revolution that broke out in February 1917 wasn't promoted by the Communists. Instead, it was the people of Petrograd who gathered in the streets to demonstrate against the autocratic power of the tsar and demanded a stop to the war. The tsar sent the army to repress the people, but instead, the army turned against him. It was the beginning of the end of tsarism.

The tsar was removed from power, and the revolutionaries installed a provisional government in his place. Trotsky was the leader of the Bolshevik Party and led the radicalization of the revolution. The Communists organized Soviets—popular assemblies—in each city and were in virtual control of power. Meanwhile, Lenin was in Germany and made an arrangement with the government to let him come back to his country. In exchange, Lenin offered to take Russia out of the war. Since the Germans desperately needed to fight the war on only one front, the authorities agreed and allowed Lenin to go to neutral Sweden, and from there, reached Russia.

He arrived in Petrograd in April 1917. Then, he led the second stage of the revolution and proposed that only the Soviets had the power. Later, the Bolsheviks took power within the Soviets in every city. By October of that year, Lenin deposed the provisional government and seized power to install a dictatorship of the proletarians. In 1918, Lenin, consequent with his original ideas and accomplishing his commitment to the German government, signed peace at Brest-Litovsk. Russia was out of World War I, and it would be a turning point in the conflict.

Meanwhile, Lenin's arrival in power sparked a civil war. Leon Trotsky had been appointed as foreign commissar by the provisional government, but after the exit of Russia from the war, he was back in Petrograd. There, Lenin gave him the order to organize the Red Army. It would be the revolutionary army to confront the supporters of the deposed government and the reminiscence of the tsarist regime. By 1920, Trotsky's Red Army had successfully repressed all the opposition to the Bolshevik revolution, and Lenin's power was ensured.

Once the Bolshevik regime was safe, Trotsky wanted to continue spreading the revolution. He had always been an advocate for internationalism. If the revolution didn't reach every corner of the capitalist world, then it wasn't the triumph of the revolution and Communism. Instead, Lenin decided they would focus on establishing a strong regime within their own country. He also believed the revolution should reach every worker in the world, but so far, they had a lot to do. It was the first Socialist regime in history ever (with a small experiment in Paris in 1869), and they had to create it.

Lenin and Trotsky had always had ideological differences, especially regarding their strategies. Once in power, those differences deepened. Nonetheless, Trotsky continued to have significant influence within the party. In 1922, Lenin suffered his first cerebral hemorrhage, and the members of the party opened the discussion about his successor. The other natural leader of the movement was indeed Leon Trotsky, but he had earned many detractors due to his intransigent ideas about the course the revolution should follow.

When Lenin died in 1924, another man had emerged in the Communist Party and gained enough support to replace the leader instead of Trotsky. His name was Joseph Stalin. After Lenin's death, Stalin seized power, and Trotsky became a state enemy. The secret police started his persecution, and he suffered many attacks. In 1928, his own party exiled him to Central Asia as once did the autocratic regime he fought to destroy. The next year, he was banned from the territory of what was by then the USSR.

After leaving his homeland, Trotsky tried to rebuild the Communist Party in Europe but was forced to constantly flee and avoid attempts to kill him. In 1940, he was hiding in Mexico, where he was attacked by two armed men. He survived the first attack, but as he was in recovery, a Spanish socialist who lived with him struck him with an ice pick.

Regardless of the consequences of the Socialist regime imposed after the revolution, Lenin and Trotsky must be credited for leaving one of the most important political phenomena of the 20th century. With rights and wrongs, they represented a different way to see the world and gave workers and the propertyless the hope of a fairer system. If they didn't achieve it, they at least left a legacy of struggle.

Nelson Mandela and Desmond Tutu (1900s)

During the last decades of the 19th century, the European powers traveled beyond their borders, searching for new territories to find a workforce and new markets and resources. Then, they reached and occupied Eastern Asia and Africa. The European countries established colonial empires. One of them, arguably the greatest of all, was Great Britain, and one of their most important possessions was a colony at the southern extreme of the continent: present-day South Africa.

The colonial occupation and British administration of the lands can be traced back to the 18th century, and it encompassed a lot of political conflicts and civil wars throughout the centuries. However, to tell the story of this duo, it is enough to refer to the last period of the colonial era that started in 1910. Under the British government, the population of South Africa became segregated. The White people and the original inhabitants of the country didn't have the same rights. The dominant White minority had established the apartheid regime that imposed racial segregation on the non-White majority. Two men would stand up and raise their voices against this cruel regime against human dignity. They were Nelson Mandela and Desmond Tutu.

One of them led to politics, and the other chose the path of religion. The first moved from pacifism to action, and the other continued to preach for peace. They had many different ideas, but they both agreed on the main purpose: to end apartheid and build for South African people a land of freedom and justice.

Nelson Rolihlahla Mandela was his name, but his people later called him "Madyba": The father of the nation. He was born on December 18, 1918, in Mvezo. In South Africa, the Western social organization coexisted with the traditional tribal structures. Nelson's father was the chief of the Tembu community. At his death, Nelson inherited the chieftaincy, but he declined it to study law at the University of the Witwatersrand.

Soon after graduation, Nelson became engaged with the nationalist cause of the African National Congress (ANC), a group that searched for the liberation of the country. In 1944, he became the leader of the Youth League. Later, he moved to Johannesburg and practiced law. He wanted to do something against the apartheid regime that forbade non-White people from moving around without certain documentation and were banned from certain places. He traveled across the country, encouraging people to rebel against those laws in a nonviolent way. He was a promoter of civil disobedience.

In 1960, the police massacred a group of Black South Africans who weren't carrying arms. That was a turning point in Mandela's political activism. He decided to leave nonviolent means and turned to more aggressive actions. He promoted sabotage against the government and went to Algeria to receive training in *guerrilla* tactics. In 1963, he was imprisoned with other men accused of subversive underground activities. In 1964, Mandela received a sentence of life imprisonment.

He was incarcerated at Robben Island Prison, off Cape Town, between 1964 and 1982, and later taken to another prison. During those years, his name became more popular and a symbol of the struggle against oppression. Meanwhile, another figure arose as an advocate for Black people's rights: Desmond Tutu.

His full name was Desmond Mpilo Tutu, and he was born on October 7, 1931, in Klerksdorp, South Africa. His father was a schoolteacher, so Desmond was educated at mission schools. He wanted to be a doctor, but his family couldn't afford the expenses, so he also became a teacher. In 1957, he moved to Johannesburg and entered St. Peter's Theological College, where he was ordained as an Anglican priest. He was the first Black South African to be appointed as a dean in the country. He was assigned to St. Mary's Cathedral in Johannesburg.

In 1978, he became the secretary of the South African Council of Churches and used his place to speak in favor of Black people's rights and against the apartheid. As Mandela did at first, he encouraged people to engage in nonviolent protests and called the other countries of the world to use economic measures to press on the government so they would retreat from the apartheid policy. In 1984, he received the Nobel Peace Prize for his activism against the apartheid. Two years later, he became the first Black archbishop in the country.

Mandela and Tutu fought their entire life the same fight but through different paths. They had met when they were young, when Desmond was a student at the university. They would meet again 40 years later when Mandela was released from prison after 27 years in jail.

When Mandela came out of prison in 1990, his name was popular among the South African population and in the international community. He represented the claim for the end of apartheid. Shortly after achieving freedom, Nelson Mandela was elected president of the ANC party and started negotiations with the government to establish a real democratic system. In 1993, he received the Nobel Peace Prize along with the current president of the nation, Frederik Willem de Klerk.

In 1994, Nelson Mandela was elected president of the country in free popular elections held for the first time in history in South Africa. His government was characterized by searching for ethnic integration and social peace. He established the Truth and Reconciliation Commission to investigate the crimes against human rights during the apartheid. There is no peace and justice without truth. The president of the commission was Desmond Tutu.

Tutu never stopped his advocacy for equal rights for all the population. He promoted the idea of South Africa as "The Rainbow Nation." When Mandela assumed his role as president, Tutu was very critical of the government and the performance of many members of the ANC party. However, Mandela always appreciated his opinions and turned back to him for advice as a good friend.

After retiring from their respective positions in public office, both men continued to be linked to international organizations in defense of human rights. It is undeniable that Nelson Mandela and Desmond Tutu contributed to making this world a better place. Their message of peace and human dignity transcended the frontiers of their country and will live forever.

Fidel Castro and Che Guevara (1900s)

For some, they were heroes who fought to build a better world. For others, they were included in the list of most sought terrorists in the world. Coming from completely different backgrounds, Fidel Castro and Che Guevara didn't have a common goal at first. But then, history put them together on the same path to lead the first successful Communist revolution in America and establish a Socialist regime in Cuba in times when the world was divided into West and East during the Cold War. Together, they confronted the autocratic regime of Batista, and later the powerful United States. Then, their paths separated again, like it happened with Lenin and Trotsky. They had different visions of how the revolution should continue.

Fidel Alejandro Castro Ruz was born on August 13, 1926. His father was a farmer who worked in a sugar company owned by a company from the United States. The region where he lived had been under US control for a long time. During his time in college, he became an excelling athlete, but his interests would turn to politics.

In 1945, he was a law student at the University of La Habana. He joined a revolutionary group formed by Cuban and Dominican students who planned to invade the Dominican Republic to overthrow the regime of dictator Trujillo. Later, he became a member of the Cuban Communist Party.

By the 1950s, Cuba was under the dictatorship of Fulgencio Batista, who had seized power through a *coup d'etat* in 1952. Fidel Castro and his brother, Raul Castro, organized the revolutionary group that attempted to overthrow Batista in a military barrack in Santiago de Cuba. The operation was a complete failure, and most of the 160 men led by the Castro brothers were killed by the army. Those who survived were imprisoned, including Raul and Fidel. The Castro brothers were released in 1955 under an amnesty law but were forced to exile in Mexico. There, they would outline a new plan against Batista.

During their stay in Mexico, Fidel met a young Argentinian medicine student. His name was Ernesto Guevara de la Serna, but everybody called him "Che," a typical word used in Argentina to refer to people. Ernesto belonged to a middle-class family from Santa Fe province. He was born on June 14, 1928. His first approach to Marxist ideas was during an adventure trip with his friend Alberto Granado. They traveled through Latin America on his motorcycle called "La Poderosa."

During his trip, Ernesto had the opportunity to see the poor living conditions of the population in many countries of Latin America. After the end of his trip, he went to Guatemala. There, he witnessed how the Socialist regime of Arbenz was overthrown by forces supported by the U.S. CIA (Sinclair, 2023). Ernesto Guevara was then persuaded that the only chance for people was to establish a Socialist system.

Later, Ernesto traveled to Mexico, where he met Fidel Castro and the revolutionary group he led. It was called "Movimiento 26 de Julio."

Along with his brother and Camilo Cienfuegos, Castro planned to come back to Cuba, invade the island, and seize power. Movimiento 26 de Julio was formed by 80 members. Ernesto heard the plan and believed the revolutionaries had no chance of success. Fidel asked him to join them. Ernesto's knowledge of medicine would be a great help during the war. They were determined to fight a guerrilla war until Batista declined power.

Eventually, Che accepted to join the Cuban revolutionaries. On December 2, 1956, Movimiento 26 de Julio crossed the Caribbean Sea on a yacht called Granma. They disembarked on the eastern coast, but the Cuban army opened fire against them. Only nine of them survived, including Fidel, his brother, and Che, who had been wounded. They hid in the thick forest of Sierra Maestra. They remained there for two years. During that time, they recruited volunteers to join the guerrilla army among the peasants who lived and worked in the region. They could survive thanks to the help the local communities gave them.

Castro and Guevara organized a guerrilla war. They assaulted military barracks or police stations to arm their people and threaten the government. By the end of 1958, Batista's regime was declining. Fidel's army of 800 people was stronger than the 30,000 professional soldiers of the Cuban state. Batista fled from Cuba, and on January 1, 1959, Fidel and Che reached the capital of the country. The revolution had succeeded.

Once in power, Fidel Castro established a Socialist regime and embodied an anti-United States policy that, in times of the Cold War, was perceived as a serious menace to the interests of the North American country. Later, Castro established an alliance with the Soviet Union, and in 1962, the missile crisis was one of the tensest points of the global conflict.

Despite the initial reforms that were aligned with people's needs, Castro's government turned into a dictatorship, and he retained power for over 40 years, only to be replaced by his brother Raul in 2006.

Ernesto Guevara supported Castro during the first years of his government. He was the industry minister and the voice of the new regime in front of the world. However, he became disappointed as he saw how Cuba became a client of the Soviet Union and the regime didn't look like the Socialist society he had dreamed of. He left the island in an attempt to promote a revolution in other countries following the same guerrilla tactic they used in Sierra Maestra. He spent time in the present-day Democratic Republic of Congo, though his attempt was a failure.

In 1966, Guevara settled in the region of Santa Cruz, Bolivia, to organize a revolutionary army. In the context of the Cold War, Guevara represented the real threat of Communism within America. Therefore, public forces of the entire continent were in pursuit of him. Guevara spent over a year hiding in the mountains, but he didn't have the positive outcomes he expected. He didn't find the same support among the Bolivian peasants as Fidel and himself found among the Cubans. By the middle of 1967, Guevara and his few partners were running away from the Bolivian army.

On October 8, 1967, the Bolivian army finally found Guevara and his people guided by information provided by the CIA. Most of his comrades were killed, and Che was wounded. He was taken prisoner only to be later executed. His body was secretly buried, and his hands were cut off. His captors wanted to keep his fingerprints to prove his identity.

The socialist regime that was installed in Cuba after the revolution has endured over 60 years, fluctuating from deep social and economic reformations to international claims of lack of liberty and political rights. The figures of Fidel and Che are controversial but will always be linked to the romantic idea of a revolution that would free the deprived from oppression, and establish a system based on equality.

Chapter 6:

Wartime Duos

Franklin D. Roosevelt and Winston Churchill (1900s)

World War II started in 1939 and lasted for almost seven years. It was the deadliest armed conflict in all of humankind's history. Every corner of the world was involved in it in one way or another. Millions of people died, and entire populations had their homes and lives changed forever.

In the middle of the war, it was almost impossible to visualize the end of the conflict, and even more complex to imagine the scenery for the moment when everything was over. Even though war is fought on the battlefields, the decisions behind the movements to attack or retreat, to negotiate or not, were in the hands of political leaders. Among them, on both sides of the Atlantic Ocean, two men had to plan a strategy not only to bring WWII to an end but also to set the foundation of the world that would seek permanent peace. President Roosevelt from the United States and Winston Churchill, Prime Minister of the United Kingdom, were those two men.

Franklin Delano Roosevelt was born on January 30, 1882, in New York. After studying law for two years and working for a Wall Street firm, Franklin found out his real interests were in politics. He was elected to take a seat in the Senate for the Democratic Party before he was 29 years old.

In 1921, his life took a dramatic turn when he was infected with poliomyelitis. His body was completely paralyzed for some time, but after a slow recovery, he was able to return to his political activity. However, he had to use a wheelchair for the rest of his life. It was never an impediment for him, and he delivered a strong message of resilience to the citizens.

Roosevelt was elected president for the first time in 1933 and remained until 1945. He is the only president of the United States to occupy the office for three terms and voted in consecutive elections. He had to lead the country through two of the greatest crises in history: the Great Depression and WWII. In 1933, Roosevelt was the promoter of the New Deal, the political and economic plan that reshaped the whole system and allowed the country to overcome the havoc left by the crash of 1929.

Later, he had to lead the country as one of the Allies to fight against the Japanese expansion and the world threat represented by Nazism. Roosevelt had to work together with the Prime Minister of the most important ally in Europe, Great Britain, in order to stop Hitler and prepare the world for the post-war period.

The prime minister of Great Britain was another influential politician in the international realm. His name was Sir Winston Leonard Spencer Churchill. He was born on November 30, 1874, in Blenheim Palace, Oxfordshire. He devoted his entire life to serving his country within its borders and abroad. He was a veteran of war and had been involved in the administration of the British colonial possessions, but he was an innate statesman. All his career prior to 1940 prepared him to lead his country during WWII.

He reached the prime minister's office in 1940 after Chamberlain's dismissal when the Germans invaded the Low Countries. Churchill, at the time, was Admiralty. Until then, Great Britain had adopted the appeasement policy against Nazi Germany to avoid leading the nation to another war. In 1940, Churchill had to make the unpopular decision to enter World War II as it was evident Hitler wouldn't stop and would eventually attempt to invade the island.

With France occupied by the Nazis, Churchill knew that the only powerful ally they could turn to was the United States, even when they hadn't entered the war. Therefore, Churchill established close diplomatic and later military relationships with his peers from the US. Together, they had to arrange and lead all the military operations to remove the Germans from France and force their retreat.

During the war, Europe's situation was complex. Germany controlled almost all of Western Continental Europe, and in the East, it fought against the Soviet regime led by Stalin. Churchill put the ideological differences aside and reached out to the Soviet Union to gather forces against the common enemy. In 1942, he traveled to Moscow to meet Stalin and discuss with him an alliance with the United States.

Churchill and Roosevelt sat at the negotiation table with Stalin to decide and plan together the strategy to defeat Hitler. Stalin proposed to land in France and make them retreat, and Roosevelt supported the motion. Churchill considered it too risky, but in the end, it was the approved plan. It resulted in the costly but successful disembarkment in Normandy on June 6, 1944, the attack that marked the beginning of the end of WWII.

In February 1945, Roosevelt and Churchill gathered in Yalta with Stalin. The Conference of Yalta was the first step for the organization of the United Nations and a new global order that persists today. Despite the insurmountable differences among the three leaders, they prioritized the creation of the instruments to prevent a new armed conflict of such a terrible scale.

Franklin Roosevelt and Winston Churchill were forced to lead their countries for the sake of the rest of the world in unknown circumstances. They had to design a new world that had never existed. They had to deal with foreign enemies, but also many detractors in their own nations because many of the decisions they had to make were controversial, and only history would prove if they had taken the correct ones.

Roosevelt had the courage to take extreme measures to save the U.S. economy from the debacle. Increasing public spending and controlling production and trade were controversial decisions within a free-trade system. He was sharply questioned for turning the country into a welfare state. However, he was able to rebuild trust among the population and construct political alliances to support a government that could navigate the crisis. In the international field, he was a fierce defender of democracy and one of the mentors of the new world order.

Churchill, on his end, was responsible for articulating the Allied powers to bring back peace and unity to Europe. While the rest of the political leaders wanted to turn their back on the war, they had the courage to see the need to intervene and fight for peace. He was one of the first leaders to think of a united Europe and sow the seed of his vision.

General Eisenhower and General Montgomery (1900s)

In 1944, the scenery in Europe was catastrophic. The Nazi regime, led by Adolf Hitler, controlled most parts of the continent. Despite the surrender of the Fascist regime of Mussolini in Italy, the end of the war still seemed to be far from being reached. While in the East, the German expansion had halted, and the Soviet Union had reverted the attack; in the West, there was little hope for the Allies.

Joseph Stalin and Franklin Roosevelt agreed on the need to implement a massive attack on the German troops. It was a suicide mission, but it was perhaps the only chance the Allies had to defeat the Nazis, recover France, and make them retreat. Eventually, Churchill accepted the challenge. On June 6, 1944, the Allied forces launched "Operation Overlord." The mission was led by the Supreme Commander of the Allied forces, General Dwight D. Eisenhower from the United States, and put into action by General Bernard L. Montgomery from Great Britain (*History through the viewfinder*, 2019).

Dwight David Eisenhower was born on October 14, 1890, in Denison, Texas. His family and friends called him "Ike." He started his military career at the U.S. Military Academy of West Point in New York in 1910. During World War I, Dwight was promoted to captain after successfully leading a tank training center, although he didn't go to the battlefield. The war ended not long before he was sent overseas.

His first important mission abroad was between 1922 and 1924, when he was appointed to command the U.S. operations in the Panama Canal Zone. There, he received the influence and teachings from Brig. Gen. Fox Conner, who was assigned to enter the Command and General Staff School at Fort Leavenworth. Later, Dwight also developed his military and leadership skills under the command of another great figure of the U.S. forces, Gen. Douglas MacArthur. Eisenhower accompanied MacArthur to the Philippines to organize the Commonwealth's army.

He came back to his country shortly after the outbreak of World War II. He achieved the rank of colonel after organizing training activities for 500,000 troops. That was proof of his ability to plan and implement complex strategies. All these previous experiences and contact with prominent military leaders prepared him well to command the most important military operation in history. However, when Operation Overlord was being prepared, he had a delay, and by January 1944, he hadn't reached London yet. Fortunately, a British commander was in charge of following his orders and preparing the troops.

This British commander was Bernard Law Montgomery. He was born on November 17, 1887, in London. He entered the military when he was very young and was a veteran of World War I, in which he was wounded twice and awarded for his courageous and efficient leadership.

When World War II broke out, Bernard actively participated throughout the conflict. First, he was assigned to invade France, and, later, to command the evacuation of the Allied troops from Dunkirk. Back in Great Britain, he was in charge of organizing the resistance in preparation for a potential German invasion of the island.

Montgomery's actions were pertinent enough to catch the attention of Prime Minister Winston Churchill, and he was appointed to command the mission in North Africa to fight against the German forces in Tunisia, where the Nazis eventually surrendered in 1943. Later, Montgomery served under Eisenhower for the first time in the invasion of Sicily in July 1943. That mission was responsible for tearing down the Fascist regime of Mussolini and was a turning point in the war in 1944. It was the first important defeat for the Axis powers.

Nonetheless, the German occupation of the rest of the continent was still an issue. Then, the Allied leaders decided on another invasion, this time against the Germans and by the North.

Then, Eisenhower started planning Operation Overlord. He had been appointed by General Marshall to command all the operations of the United States Army in Europe and had already led the invasion of French North Africa. He took charge of the impossible mission of invading Northern France under the heavy fire of the Germans. He knew it would cost the lives of thousands of Allied soldiers, but still, there was no other choice if they wanted to end the war. The day before the attack, he wrote a message taking full responsibility if the mission failed.

Eisenhower didn't plan the invasion alone. General Montgomery was with him and provided his opinions, which were listened to and mostly accepted by the U.S. general. However, the relationship between the two men was often tense because Montgomery had an arrogant personality. Once, Eisenhower had to remind him he was his chief and that he should be treated with respect (*History through the viewfinder*, 2019). Nonetheless, Eisenhower trusted Montgomery's expertise and experience, and his view and skills were of utmost relevance to planning the attack through the English Channel.

The plan was to cross the English Channel with a large number of soldiers and invade Normandy. The objective was to carry out a surprise attack, so there was a distraction operation carried out to the North of the real point set for the disembarkment. The troops would land between Caen and the Cotentin peninsula. The Allies would send three divisions that would cross the channel, and two brigades would be dropped from the air. Initially, Eisenhower had decided to send five divisions by ship, but Montgomery suggested an amphibious attack and reducing the land divisions to three (*History through the viewfinder*, 2019). During the following weeks, 11 divisions, mainly from the United States, would land, and once the foothold was ensured, they would move through France to reach the German border.

On June 6th, the Allied troops crossed the channel and landed in Normandy. Eisenhower had set June 5th to start the operation. After his order, 3,000 landing crafts, 2,500 ships, and 500 escorts and bombardment ships sailed through the English Channel to the French coast. At night, 822 aircraft took off from British shores with the soldiers equipped with parachutes to be dropped on the Normandy shore. In total, 150,000 soldiers landed on D-Day in Normandy. That very day, over 4,400 Allied soldiers were killed, and more than 5,000 were wounded (*Remembering D-Day*, 2023).

The combat continued in the days that followed, and the number of casualties rose to 73,000 soldiers dead and 150,000 wounded. The military advance and the German response spread through villages in the French territory, leaving the horrifying record of 20,000 French civilians dead (*Remembering D-Day*, 2023). The costs of the invasion were indeed high and painful. However, if Eisenhower hadn't made that terribly difficult decision, the Allies would have experienced a long dominance of Germany on the continent, and it is impossible to know how long the conflict would have endured.

If Eisenhower is the one to be credited for the decision and the diligent leadership of the operation under the most terrible circumstances, Montgomery was the one in charge on the battlefield. He commanded all the ground forces in Normandy that D-Day morning. After the successful first stage of invasion, Montgomery led the Allied troops through France, Belgium, and the Netherlands, and entered Germany on May 4, 1945. He was at Lüneburg Heath when he received the formal capitulation of the German Army (Keegan, 2023).

After the end of the war, Montgomery was awarded a Knight of the Garter and became 1st Viscount Montgomery of Alamein in 1946. Nonetheless, he continued to serve the British Army during the following years. His experience on the field and his personal achievements gained him a place in the Western European Union defense organization and as a commander of the NATO headquarters (Keegan, 2023).

On his end, Dwight Eisenhower was elected president of the United States after the war, in 1953. During his mandate, he had to approach the Communist leader Joseph Stalin and negotiate the end of the Korean War in 1953. In the complex context of the Cold War and under the real threat of a potentially mass destruction nuclear war, he promoted the "open skies" policy. He proposed that all the atomic information and materials were under the auspice of an international organization to ensure peace. That was eventually agreed upon at the Geneva Conference in 1955. That was a major step to building a safer world.

Anne Frank and Miep Gies (1900s)

The Nazi party and its leader, Adolf Hitler, seized power in 1933. Until then, it was hard to imagine that human beings could be capable of the horror they unleashed on the Jewish population and many others. Never before in all of humankind's history has a state used its power and resources to build death machinery dedicated to eliminating part of the population. After World War II ended, evidence found in the concentration and death camps showed the world what the Nazis were doing. Over six million people were forced to live in inhuman conditions, suffered torture and harassment, and were executed in cold blood.

Even though the numbers and the records of the camps are proof enough of how terrible Nazism was, nothing is more moving than hearing the testimonies of those who survived. However, one of the most worldwide renowned testimonies came from someone who didn't survive. Anne Frank detailed her memories of the Holocaust from the inside, from the perspective of a teenager, through the pages of her diary. Her narration, in fact, told about her life before she was taken to the concentration camp, and that way, it reminds the world that the Holocaust began for the victims far before they became prisoners.

Annelies Marie Frank was born to a Jewish family on June 12, 1929, in Frankfurt am Main. Her father, Otto, decided to take his family out of Germany when Hitler seized power and the first antisemitic laws were passed. The Franks moved to Amsterdam. Eventually, the Nazis invaded the Netherlands, and the rules against the Jews reached them there. Anne was forced to leave her school and attend a new one only for Jewish children.

On her 13th birthday, she received a red and white diary as a present. She wrote on the first page: "I hope I will be able to confide everything to you, as I have never been able to confide in anyone, and I hope you will be a great source of comfort and support" (Berenbaum, 2023, para. 2). It was a few days before Anne's life changed forever.

On July 6th, Anne's sister, Margot, was searched by the Gestapo to be deported. By then, there were rumors about what happened to the Jews when they were taken by the Nazi police. However, Anne's family sought a place to hide to avoid being caught by them. There weren't a lot of people willing to help the Jews because that made them potential victims of the Nazi regime as well. However, Anne and her family found a woman who didn't mind risking her own life to help them. Her name was Miep Gies.

Miep was an office worker at Otto Frank's company. When he found out his daughter was in danger, he asked Miep to hide them. On July 6, 1942, Anne, her family, and another Jewish family entered the warehouse at the back of the food factory owned by Frank. The two families would spend two years hiding in a secret annex at Prinsengracht 263.

Anne and her family couldn't have survived if they didn't have a few friends like Miep, who assisted them. During those two years, they never left the room. They had to remain enclosed and even keep silent during the day while the rest of the people were at the office to avoid anyone suspecting them. The only way they could have the supplies they needed to survive was through friends like Miep. She smuggled food and other essentials to provide for the Franks. Every time she walked through the streets carrying the goods, she risked being discovered.

During her time inside the annex, Anne wrote in her diary. She talked about daily issues but also about her feelings as a teenager and the fear of being found by the Nazis. The last entry of the diary is dated August 1, 1944. Three days later, somebody gave Anne and her family away to the Gestapo, and the Nazis discovered the annex. The Franks, the other family hiding with them, and two of the people who helped them were arrested.

Anne and her sister were driven to Auschwitz, one of the extermination camps in Poland, occupied by the Nazis by then. Later, both girls were transferred to Bergen-Belsen. Anne and her sister were infected with typhus during an epidemic in the camp, which was very common due to the weak condition of the inmates and the extremely unhygienic conditions. Anne died in March 1945, just a few weeks before the war ended, and the Allied troops reached the camp to free the prisoners.

When the Nazis discovered the annex and arrested Anne and her family, they also raided Miep's apartment. However, Miep Gies managed to hide Anne's diary and kept it secret until the war ended. Later, she met Otto, the only member of the family who survived, and gave him his daughter's diary back. Otto decided to publish the diary under the title *Anne Frank: The Diary of a Young Girl*.

The book was originally published in Dutch but has been translated into 65 languages. It is the most read book about the Holocaust. Its legacy will survive over generations because it is the depiction of life and hope in the middle of the horrors of war and persecution through the pure eyes of a child.

Chester Nimitz and Douglas MacArthur (1900s)

Certainly, the 20th century was scarred by armed conflicts. Historian Eric Hobsbawm called it the "era of the catastrophes" (Hobsbawm, 1994). It was already told how Eisenhower and Montgomery were credited with ensuring the Allied victory on the West front in Europe during World War II, but the war was also fought in another hot spot. The Pacific Ocean was the chosen field for the imperial expansion of one of the belligerent countries of the Axis powers: Japan. After the attack on the U.S. Naval Base in Pearl Harbor, the battles in the islands and waters of the Pacific began. It was of utmost importance to force the Japanese to retreat not only to stop their expansion but also to demoralize the troops and eventually force them to surrender.

Douglas MacArthur was born on January 26, 1880, in Little Rock, Arkansas. He graduated with honors from military school and served in the army abroad in the country when he was very young. By 1930, he had reached the rank of general. In 1935, he was appointed to reorganize the defense of the Philippine Islands, but despite this important endeavor, he retired from the U.S. Army in 1937.

Nonetheless, after World War II began, he was called from retirement to come back to duty. And so, he did. He was first sent to the Philippines, and later to Australia to organize the counteroffensive against the Japanese that had bombarded Pearl Harbor in 1941 and continued to occupy the islands in the Pacific Ocean. MacArthur was in charge of the military operations in the Southwest Pacific. Despite his talent to command military operations and his experience on the battlefield, MacArthur had a tough personality and often questioned his superiors' orders. He considered that the Allies had prioritized the war in Europe and relegated the Pacific theater of operations, underestimating Japan as a dangerous and ambitious enemy.

With fewer resources than he would have liked, MacArthur held a heroic resistance in the Pacific islands. He outlined the strategy to undermine the naval supremacy that Japan had at the first stage of the war. However, MacArthur could only carry out his strategy and obtain the first victories, the key to keeping the morale of his troops up, thanks to one of his admirals, Nimitz, the chief of the fleet.

Chester Nimitz was born on February 24, 1885, in Fredericksburg, Texas. Being a commander of the Navy, he led troops by sea and on land during World War II. He was distinguished for his courage and skills as a strategist. He graduated from the U.S. Naval Academy in 1905 and took part in World War I as a chief commander of the U.S. Atlantic submarine forces.

His career and excellent performance in the Navy made the authorities promote him to Chief of the Pacific Fleet right after the Japanese attack on Pearl Harbor. He was the leader of the U.S. troops who obtained the most significant victories in the campaign in the Pacific: Midway and the Coral Sea, Salomon Islands, and Iwo Jima, just to name the most popular battles.

MacArthur and Nimitz had to plan and execute their strategies with fewer resources because The Allies were focused on the war against the Nazis. Therefore, MacArthur and Nimitz developed strategies called "Island Hopping" and would bypass attacking the Japanese bases where they were weaker. MacArthur and Nimitz played leapfrog with their enemies. They used aviation forces to break the Japanese lines and leave them isolated from one group to another. It was the only opportunity the U.S. troops had to force them to retreat.

Despite the initial success of the campaigns, MacArthur and Nimitz knew that the Philippines were the key to regaining control in the Pacific. The islands had been a U.S. colony since 1898 and had failed to defend the population from the Japanese invasion in December 1941. MacArthur, who had been there trying, with little success, to organize a defense with a reduced budget, felt the United States had a moral obligation to return to the islands and free the citizens from the Japanese power.

MacArthur and Nimitz met with President Roosevelt in Pearl Harbor in July 1944 to discuss the next steps. Nimitz and MacArthur had different opinions about the last offensive against Japan. MacArthur wanted to take the Philippine Islands, while Nimitz proposed to launch the attack from Taiwan. Eventually, President Roosevelt leaned for MacArthur's proposal and convinced him that this time, he would have all the military support he needed.

The campaign to attack Japan and force Hirohito to surrender led to the final capitulation on September 2, 1945. The ceremony of surrender was led by Douglas MacArthur, and it took place in the USS *Missouri* under the command of Chester Nimitz.

After the war, Nimitz continued to serve in the U.S. Navy but only for two more years. He never accepted positions with higher salaries that would imply renouncing a lifetime appointment as a member of the Naval forces.

On his end, MacArthur was assigned to lead the U.S. occupation of Japan after the capitulation. He was in charge of the demobilization of the Japanese army, removing all the military leaders from public office, restoring the economy, and rebuilding the country. He remained in that role until 1951.

Later, he would become the commander of the United Nations forces to lead in the Korean War that broke out in 1950. His troops were defeated by the North Korean troops, but he organized the counterattack. Nonetheless, President Truman relieved him from his charge after accusing him of insubordination and making decisions without approval. When MacArthur came back to the United States, people welcomed him like a hero and supported him despite the president's decision.

Like other duos, MacArthur and Nimitz didn't share the same path to their achievements and had deep differences. Nonetheless, they were wise enough to recognize the moments when they needed each other despite those differences and to prioritize the goals they both fought for. If they hadn't continued to fight in the Pacific while the Allies turned their back on this war scenario, Japan would have probably ensured its positions and the war would have been prolonged, causing more casualties and loss. They failed and made a lot of mistakes, but that is what happens to those who dare make decisions and are ready to be accountable for the consequences. Those who never dare to do so don't get to be remembered by history.

Conclusion

Can one person change the world? Throughout these pages, it has been shown that if a person can't change the world by a single effort, having an accomplice to join forces can contribute to leaving enduring footprints. All the people in this book lived extraordinary lives and somehow turned the course of the history of humankind. Some did it through their contributions to science, others engaged in social movements. Others simply transcended the powerful message of self-overcoming and surpassing the limits of their times. All of these stories have profound lessons to teach us.

Some of these duos have been captured by popular imagination as unforgettable names, while others haven't received fair treatment from history. While some names kept the plaudits, their partners remained in the shadows. This book aimed to tell the stories of some whose names come to mind together immediately, and also give some credit to those who were relegated. Thanks to this book, readers now know that even geniuses can thrive if they have a partner to support them.

It is difficult to know if all of them could have achieved any of their accomplishments on their own. It is proved that together, they went even further than they might have alone. It is the synergy that arises when two people with common interests and similar dreams make the impossible happen.

They found obstacles in their way, and they had to work together to overcome them. And surely, knowing there is someone ready to support them is key to never giving up and continuing to fight. Many of the stories shared here are testimonies of resilience and dealing with extreme challenges. It is always better when there is a helping hand at one's side.

Each story of the duos is framed in a particular historical context. The surrounding circumstances determined their goals and also worked to bring these people together. At the same time, by the joint effort to accomplish those goals, these duos helped to shape the contemporary world. It doesn't matter if their contributions date from centuries ago—all of them have left an enduring legacy that continues to build the present and keeps inspiring new generations. They have paved the way for future developments and progress.

Each of the names included in these chapters is worthy of admiration, but the names put together in duos become a source of motivation and inspiration. They have shown us that the power of collaboration and partnership is limitless, and finding the perfect match is the key to achieving extraordinary things.

Have you found your perfect match to overcome challenges and thrive? Would you be willing to share the glory of a great accomplishment with a partner? Perhaps that goal you have been trying to achieve is just waiting for you to find someone who can boost the synergy that will bring forth the best version of yourself.

Once a secret of success is unraveled, the right thing to do is to share it. Regular people doing great things are eventually the ones that change the world. Leave a review and share this thriving secret with as many people as possible and be part of that change. Perhaps this is how you will find the perfect match for your duo.

References

Abernathy, Ralph David. (n.d.). The Martin Luther King, Jr. Research and Education Institute. https://kinginstitute.stanford.edu/abernathy-ralph-david#:~:text=While%20a%20graduate%20student%20at,%E2%80%9D%20(Abernathy%2C%2089)

Albert Einstein–Biographical. (n.d.). Nobel Prize. https://www.nobelprize.org/prizes/physics/1921/einstein/biographical/

Anderson, G. (2021, July 30). *Who was La Malinche?* Smithsonian Magazine. https://www.smithsonianmag.com/smart-news/was-la-malinche-indigenous-interpreter-conquistador-hernan-cortes-traitor-survivor-or-icon-180978321/

Badian, E., Grant, M. & Others. (2023, July 28). *Mark Antony.* Encyclopaedia Britannica. https://www.britannica.com/biography/Mark-Antony-Roman-triumvir

Bevington, D. (2023, August 14). *Romeo and Juliet.* Encyclopedia Britannica. https://www.britannica.com/topic/Romeo-and-Juliet.

Berenbaum, M. (2023, August 18). *Anne Frank.* Encyclopedia Britannica. https://www.britannica.com/biography/Anne-Frank

Buckley, J. H. (2023a, August 14). *Meriwether Lewis.* Encyclopedia Britannica. https://www.britannica.com/biography/Meriwether-Lewis

Buckley, J. H. (2023b, August 28). *William Clark*. Encyclopedia Britannica. https://www.britannica.com/biography/William-Clark

Buckley, J. H. (2023c, September 5). *Lewis and Clark Expedition*. Encyclopedia Britannica. https://www.britannica.com/event/Lewis-and-Clark-Expedition

Caballero, M. (2016, March 19). *Marie Curie and the discovery of radioactivity*. Stanford University. http://large.stanford.edu/courses/2016/ph241/caballero2/#:~:text=%5B2%5D%20Curie%20worked%20on%20the,accurate%20and%20stronger%20x%2Drays

Carlton, G. (2022, April 23). *The little-known story Of Mileva Marić, Albert Einstein's first wife and tragically overlooked partner*. All That's Interesting. https://allthatsinteresting.com/mileva-maric

Daniels, R.V. (2023, September 17). *Leon Trotsky*. Encyclopedia Britannica. https://www.britannica.com/biography/Leon-Trotsky

Dead Wild Roses. (2019, September 28). *Tagged with Simone de Beauvoir*. https://deadwildroses.com/tag/simone-de-beauvoir/

The Declaration of Sentiments (U.S). (2023, March 29). National Park Service. https://www.nps.gov/articles/declaration-of-sentiments.htm#:~:text=Elizabeth%20Cady%20Stanton%20wrote%20the,gender%20inequality%20in%20the%20U.S

Del Campo, M. (2019, May 24). *"Soyez réalistes, demandez l'impossible" May 1968 France*. European Collections. https://europeancollections.wordpress.com/2019/05/24/soyez-realistes-demandez-limpossible-may-1968-france/#:~:text=%E2%80%9CBe%20realistic%2C%20ask%20the%20impossible,political%20ideas%20of%20each%20individual

Desan, W. (2023, October 5). *Jean-Paul Sartre*. Encyclopaedia Britannica. https://www.britannica.com/biography/Jean-Paul-Sartre

Encyclopaedia Britannica. (2022, December 14). *Elizabeth Cady Stanton*. https://www.britannica.com/biography/Elizabeth-Cady-Stanton

Encyclopaedia Britannica. (2023a, March 21). *Bernard Law Montgomery, 1st Viscount Montgomery*. https://www.britannica.com/biography/Bernard-Law-Montgomery-1st-Viscount-Montgomery

Encyclopaedia Britannica. (2023b, April 13). *Ralph David Abernathy*. https://www.britannica.com/biography/Ralph-David-Abernathy

Encyclopaedia Britannica. (2023c, May 18). *Simone de Beauvoir*. https://www.britannica.com/biography/Simone-de-Beauvoir

Encyclopaedia Britannica. (2023d, July 20). *Amelia Earhart*. https://www.britannica.com/biography/Amelia-Earhart

Encyclopaedia Britannica. (2023e, July 24). *Marina*. https://www.britannica.com/biography/Marina-Mexican-Native-American-princess

Encyclopaedia Britannica. (2023f, August 11). *Susan B. Anthony*. https://www.britannica.com/biography/Susan-B-Anthony

Encyclopaedia Britannica. (2023g, August 28). *Chester W. Nimitz*. https://www.britannica.com/biography/Chester-W-Nimitz

Encyclopaedia Britannica. (2023h, September 6). *Gabrielle-Émilie Le Tonnelier de Breteuil, marquise du Châtelet*. https://www.britannica.com/biography/Gabrielle-Emilie-Le-Tonnelier-de-Breteuil-Marquise-du-Chatelet

Encyclopaedia Britannica. (2023j, September 7). *Fidel Castro*. https://www.britannica.com/biography/Fidel-Castro

Encyclopaedia Britannica. (2023k, September 15). *Diego Rivera.* https://www.britannica.com/biography/Diego-Rivera

Encyclopaedia Britannica. (2023l, September 26). *Desmond Tutu.* https://www.britannica.com/biography/Desmond-Tutu

Encyclopaedia Britannica. (2023m, September 26). *Nelson Mandela.* https://www.britannica.com/biography/Nelson-Mandela

Encyclopaedia Britannica. (2023n, October 13). *Tenzing Norgay.* https://www.britannica.com/biography/Tenzing-Norgay

Eschner, K. (2021, December 17). *Five things to know about French Enlightenment genius Émilie du Châtelet.* Smithsonian Magazine. https://www.smithsonianmag.com/smart-news/five-things-know-about-french-enlightenment-genius-emilie-du-chatelet-180967561/

Esterson, A. & Cassidy, D. (2019, March 14). *Does Einstein's first wife deserve some credit for his work? That's the wrong question to ask.* Time. https://time.com/5551098/mileva-einstein-history/

Fidel Castro's military exploits and his friendship with Che Guevara. (2016, November 26). The Indian Express. https://indianexpress.com/article/world/fidel-castros-military-exploits-and-his-friendship-with-che-guevara-4396191/

Freidel, F. (2023, September 20). *Roosevelt, Franklin D.* Encyclopedia Britannica. https://www.britannica.com/biography/Franklin-D-Roosevelt

Frida Kahlo biography. (n.d.). Frida Kahlo. https://www.fridakahlo.org/frida-kahlo-biography.jsp

Hare, J. (2015, May 9). *History: An Elmira link for Helen Keller, Mark Twain.* Star Gazette. https://www.stargazette.com/story/news/local/2015/05/09/mark-twain-helen-keller-elmira/27058987/

Harmon, R. (2020, July 18). *What are the real origins of Shakespeare's "Romeo and Juliet?"* Search Medium. https://medium.com/thesmartie-newsletter/what-are-the-real-origins-of-shakespeares-romeo-and-juliet-943f56d98a3a

Hayward, N. (n.d.). *Susan B. Anthony.* National Women's History Museum. https://www.womenshistory.org/education-resources/biographies/susan-b-anthony

Hillary and Norgay reach Everest summit. (n.d.). Sky History. https://www.history.co.uk/this-day-in-history/29-may/hillary-and-norgay-reach-everest-summit

History through the viewfinder. (2019, January 11). The National WWII Museum. https://www.nationalww2museum.org/war/articles/history-through-viewfinder-44#:~:text=Montgomery%20was%20a%20difficult%20and,not

Hobsbawm, E. (1994). *The age of extremes: the short twentieth century, 1914-1991.*

Innes, R. H. (2023, August 10). *Hernán Cortés.* Encyclopedia Britannica.https://www.britannica.com/biography/Hernan-Cortes

James, D. C. (2023, August 16). *Douglas MacArthur.* Encyclopedia Britannica. https://www.britannica.com/biography/Douglas-MacArthur

Keegan, J. (2023, August 29). *Normandy Invasion.* Encyclopedia Britannica. https://www.britannica.com/event/Normandy-Invasion

Le Beau Lucchesi, E. (2022, April 27). *Three ways Cleopatra contributed to science and medicine.* Discover. https://www.discovermagazine.com/the-sciences/three-ways-cleopatra-contributed-to-science-and-medicine

Lewis & Clark expedition. (2021, June 1). National Archives. https://www.archives.gov/education/lessons/lewis-clark#background

Library of the Congress. (n.d.). *Elizabeth Cady Stanton papers.* https://www.loc.gov/collections/elizabeth-cady-stanton-papers/about-this-collection/

Lucas, K. (2019, October 29). *Meet Émilie du Châtelet, the French socialite who helped lay the foundations of modern physics.* Massive Science. https://massivesci.com/articles/gabrielle-emilie-du-chatelet-voltaire-newton-physics/

Marie Curie the scientist. (n.d.). Mariecurie.org.uk. https://www.mariecurie.org.uk/who/our-history/marie-curie-the-scientist

MacArthur Memorial education programs. (n.d.). MacArthur Memorial. https://www.macarthurmemorial.org/DocumentCenter/View/1893/Island-Hopping-Primary-Resources

McCudden, M.R., Livingston, R. & Wallenfeldt, J. (2023, August 9). *Martin Luther King, Jr., 1929–68.* Encyclopedia Britannica. *https://www.britannica.com/topic/Martin-Luther-King-Jr-1929-68-2229053.*

Meares, H. (2020, September 9). *Antony and Cleopatra's legendary love story.* Biography. https://www.biography.com/royalty/cleopatra-mark-antony-love-story-death

Meisler, S. (1986, April 16). *De Beauvoir, writer and feminist, Dies.* The New York Times. https://www.latimes.com/archives/la-xpm-1986-04-15-mn-4814-story.html

Mileva Einstein-Maric—facts, husband and life. (n.d.). Biography. https://www.biography.com/history-culture/mileva-einstein-maric

Mohammed, F. (2019, March 1). *Who was La Malinche?* JSTOR Daily. https://daily.jstor.org/who-was-la-malinche/

Mohandas Karamchand Gandhi. (2022, October 7). South African History Online. https://www.sahistory.org.za/people/mohandas-karamchand-gandhi

Monteil, A. (2022, June 26). *Amelia Earhart: the life story you may not know.* CT News Junkie. https://ctnewsjunkie.com/2022/06/26/amelia-earhart-the-life-story-you-may-not-know/#:~:text=1897%3A%20Born%20in%20Kansas&text=She%20and%20younger%20sister%20Muriel,hunting%20and%20sledding%20alongside%20Muriel

Moraes, F.R. (2023, September 24). *Jawaharlal Nehru.* Encyclopaedia Britannica. https://www.britannica.com/biography/Jawaharlal-Nehru

Nanda, B.R. (2023, September 17). *Gandhi, Mahatma.* Encyclopedia Britannica. https://www.britannica.com/biography/Mahatma-Gandhi

Nicholas, H. G. (2023, July 2). *Churchill, Winston.* Encyclopedia Britannica. https://www.britannica.com/biography/Winston-Churchill

Pierre C. (1905). Nobel lecture. https://www.nobelprize.org/uploads/2018/06/pierre-curie-lecture.pdf

Pierre Curie—biographical. (n.d.). Nobel Prize. https://www.nobelprize.org/prizes/physics/1903/pierre-curie/biographical/

Pierre Curie—death, Marie Curie and facts. (2014, April 2). Biography. https://www.biography.com/scientists/pierre-curie

Pomeau, R. Hr. (2023, August 17). *Voltaire.* Encyclopedia Britannica., https://www.britannica.com/biography/Voltaire

Rand, C. (1954, May 28). *The story of the first Sherpa to climb to the top of the Mt. Everest.* The New Yorker. https://www.newyorker.com/magazine/1954/06/05/tenzing-of-everest

Reeves, C. (2023, September 4). *Dwight D. Eisenhower.* Encyclopedia Britannica., https://www.britannica.com/biography/Dwight-D-Eisenhowe.

Remembering D-Day: Key facts and figures about epochal World War II invasion. (2023, June 5). AP News. https://apnews.com/article/d-day-invasion-normandy-france-nazis-07094640dd7bb938a23e144cc23f348c

Resis, A. (2023, June 8). *Vladimir Lenin.* Encyclopedia Britannica. https://www.britannica.com/biography/Vladimir-Lenin

Roosevelt and Churchill: a friendship that saved the world (U.S). (2015, November 17). National Park Service. https://www.nps.gov/articles/fdrww2.htm

Sartore, M. (2021, September 23). *How exactly did Anne Sullivan teach Helen Keller to communicate?* Ranker. https://www.ranker.com/list/anne-sullivan-helen-keller/melissa-sartore

The second sex and Simon de Beuvoir—One is not born, but rather becomes a Woman—Explained! (2016, December 3). Dead Wild Roses. https://deadwildroses.com/2016/12/03/the-second-sex-and-simon-de-beuvoir-one-is-not-born-but-rather-becomes-a-woman-explained/

Sinclair, A.A. (2023, June 10). *Guevara, Che.* Encyclopedia Britannica. https://www.britannica.com/biography/Che-Guevara

Sir Edmund Hillary and Tenzing Norgay—1953 Everest. (2013, March 3). National Geographic. https://www.nationalgeographic.com/adventure/article/sir-edmund-hillary-tenzing-norgay-1953

Smith, T.K., Hauk, A., & Ruhe, P. (2019, October 3). *The legacy of Mexican painter Frida Kahlo—brown, queer, disabled and revolutionary.* Arts Alt. https://www.artsatl.org/the-legacy-of-mexican-painter-frida-kahlo-brown-queer-disabled-and-revolutionary/

Solly, M. (2023, May 12). *'A small light' tells the story of Miep Gies, who hid Anne Frank from the Nazis.* https://www.smithsonianmag.com/smart-news/a-small-light-tells-the-story-of-miep-gies-who-hid-anne-frank-from-the-nazis-180982175/

"Soyez réalistes, demandez l'impossible" May 1968 France. (2019, May 24). European Collections. https://europeancollections.wordpress.com/2019/05/24/soyez-realistes-demandez-limpossible-may-1968-france/#:~:text=%E2%80%9CBe%20realistic%2C%20ask%20the%20impossible,political%20ideas%20of%20each%20individual

Teso, L. (2015, March 21). *Juliet's house in fair Verona: A sentimental journey.* Mycornerofitaly.com. https://mycornerofitaly.com/juliets-house/

Tutu & Mandela: Sometimes at odds but united against apartheid. (2021, December 21). EWN. https://ewn.co.za/2021/12/29/tutu-and-mandela-sometimes-at-odds-united-against-apartheid

Tyldesley, J. (2023, September 4). *Cleopatra.* Encyclopedia Britannica. https://www.britannica.com/biography/Cleopatra-queen-of-Egypt

Walton, G. (2018, May 30). *Voltaire and Émilie du Châtelet: Their relationship.* Geriwalton.com. https://www.geriwalton.com/voltaire-emilie-du-chatelet/

Waxman, O. (2020, December 15). *Co-founding the ACLU, fighting for labor rights and other Helen Keller accomplishments students don't learn in school.* Time. https://time.com/5918660/helen-keller-disability-history/

Who was Anne Frank? (n.d.). Anne Frank Stichting. https://www.annefrank.org/en/anne-frank/who-was-anne-frank/

Woods, A. & Grant, T. (2020, August 12). *Lenin and Trotsky—What they really stood for.* La Defence of Marxism. https://www.marxist.com/lenin-trotsky-stalinism-johnstone/appendix-a-%E2%80%93-trotsky-his-ideas.htm

Zelazko, A. (2023, September 20). *Frida Kahlo.* Encyclopedia Britannica. https://www.britannica.com/biography/Frida-Kahlo

Printed in Great Britain
by Amazon

39207788R00066